RITUALS
of
CELEBRATION

About the Author

Jane Meredith is a Priestess of the Goddess and a writer. She lives in Sydney, Australia, and presents workshops worldwide. Her interests include mythology, magic, and ritual. Her books are *Aphrodite's Magic: Celebrate and Heal Your Sexuality* and *Journey to the Dark Goddess*. You can sign up for Jane's e-zine, learn about upcoming workshops, and read more by visiting www.janemeredith.com.

To Write to the Author

If you wish to contact the author or would like more information about this book, please write to the author in care of Llewellyn Worldwide, and we will forward your request. Both the author and publisher appreciate hearing from you and learning of your enjoyment of this book and how it has helped you. Llewellyn Worldwide cannot guarantee that every letter written to the author can be answered, but all will be forwarded. Please write to:

Jane Meredith
℅ Llewellyn Worldwide
2143 Wooddale Drive
Woodbury, MN 55125-2989

Please enclose a self-addressed stamped envelope for reply,
or $1.00 to cover costs. If outside the USA, enclose
an international postal reply coupon.

Many of Llewellyn's authors have personal websites. For more information, please visit our website at http://www.llewellyn.com.

RITUALS
of
CELEBRATION

Honoring the Seasons of Life through the Wheel of the Year

Jane Meredith

Llewellyn Publications
Woodbury, Minnesota

FIRST EDITION
First Printing, 2013

Book design by Bob Gaul
Cover art: Background leaves © iStockphoto.com/Ingmar Wesemann
         Tree of Life pendant handcrafted by Ethora © www.ethora.com
Cover design by Adrienne Zimiga
Editing by Amy Quale
Interior art: Wheel of the Year illustrations © Llewellyn art department
         Tree of Life pendant handcrafted by Ethora © www.ethora.com

Llewellyn Publications is a registered trademark of Llewellyn Worldwide Ltd.

Library of Congress Cataloging-in-Publication Data
Meredith, Jane, 1964–
  Rituals of celebration: honoring the seasons of life through the wheel of the year/
Jane Meredith.—First edition
    pages cm
  ISBN 978-0-7387-3544-3
1. Rites and ceremonies. 2. Seasons—Miscellanea. 3.Wiccans. 4. Witches.
5. Neopagans. I. Title.
  BL590.M47 2013
  299'.94—dc23
                          2013008348

Llewellyn Publications
A Division of Llewellyn Worldwide Ltd.
2143 Wooddale Drive
Woodbury, MN 55125-2989
www.llewellyn.com

Printed in the United States of America

This book is dedicated
to Damon Artemis Meredith

———————

*And with thanks to the many, many people who
came to these Festivals over fifteen years, bringing
food, energy, enthusiasm, masks, candles, ribbons,
painted eggs, and the willingness to celebrate the
Eight Festivals. You created the community that
made these rituals possible.*

Contents

Spring Equinox   85

Beltaine   119

Summer Solstice   153

Lammas   187

Autumn Equinox 221

Samhain 255

Ritual Basics 295

Create Your Own Seasonal Ritual 311

Introduction

The Winter Solstice arrives at midwinter, the shortest day and longest night of the year. From now on the light gains strength day by day. It is the great turning point, the birth of the year and the new cycle.

Imbolc arrives with the realization that winter will come to an end, and is traditionally associated with lambs and the first snowdrop. It symbolizes hopes, wishes, and all new beginnings.

During the Spring Equinox, day and night are of equal length, a moment of balance before the summer months. This is the time to sow the seeds saved from the previous year, whether they are literal seeds of barley and corn or the projects and plans we've dreamed up.

Beltaine, also known as May Day, heralds the beginning of summer. Flowers and greenery abound, displaying the raw force and fertility of nature. It is a celebration of joy and sexuality.

The Summer Solstice is the longest day and shortest night, where the year hovers at its peak. Love, plenty, and the full power of the summer season are celebrated in this sacred marriage between earth and sun.

The Wheel turns again and Lammas arrives. As we begin to gather in our harvest—whether from our spiritual life, our vegetable garden, or our relationships—we recognize the hard work still to come and decide what needs to be sacrificed or discarded.

The Autumn Equinox is another day and night of equal length, and this time we face the dark half of the year. Our hard work is measured in the completed harvest and we take this opportunity to consciously turn inward.

Samhain, popularly known as Halloween, is the late evening of the year. On this night we remember and honor the dead. We submerge our awareness into the spirit realms, release whatever holds us back, and walk boldly into the dark, trusting that rebirth will occur.

These Eight Festivals make up the Wheel of the Year, a wheel that is ever turning and where each aspect forms a vital part of the whole. In celebrating the Festivals we celebrate the entire cycle of life, death, and regeneration—a cycle to which the whole of nature is bound. We come again into awareness of belonging to the earth and a deep sense of participation in the natural world.

When my son Damon turned five, I made a momentous decision.

I decided I wanted him to grow up believing that celebrating the natural cycles was an ordinary thing to do. I did not want him to think our earth-based religion was a couple of people isolated from the mainstream, connected to a few others scattered around the edges of the world. I wanted to give him an experience of security, acceptance, and belonging in a spiritual path. To do this, I had to create a context where ritual, magic, and a relationship to nature would be the norm. We already celebrated the Eight Festivals of the Wheel of the Year and I decided to try to create a community around them. I wanted him to feel that even though what we were doing might differ from the secular world all around us, or the vague Christianization of our Australian culture, our beliefs were just as valid and he was not in any way alone.

I began creating large rituals eight times a year. I invited everyone I knew, and people came; sometimes forty people were there, and sometimes eight. People came with their children, their partners, visiting brothers or sisters, friends, or parents. They brought colleagues, acquaintances, and their children's friends; once, someone brought a hitchhiker. Community activists came, and permaculturalists; feminists, people who were into yoga, healing, and conscious parenting. Some of them called themselves Pagans, but there were also Buddhists, Sanyasans, Christians, atheists, and spiritual seekers. These people wanted to be part of celebrations that were related to our season and location. They wanted to be creative, have fun, and be with others in a deep awareness of the natural cycles of their lives and the earth.

The rituals were held on the Sunday afternoons closest to the date of each Festival. Everyone present was an active part of the ritual. There were always children, from babies and toddlers to teenagers. I ran the Festivals for fifteen years, always at someone's house and always free of charge. I distributed the cost of materials by asking people to bring things, such as decorated eggs for the Spring Equinox, masks for Samhain, and ribbons and gifts at Beltaine. After a ritual we would always share a meal together. We had a Harvest Feast for the Autumn Equinox; on the Summer Solstice we celebrated with fruit; and at Samhain we had an Ancestors' Feast, making dishes traditional to our family, culture, or background.

Because one of the Eight Festivals occurs every six to eight weeks, they became part of the fabric of everyday life. I would look up and see Damon playing with a friend on the floor or talking seriously with an adult about the ritual and I could see he was comfortable and expansive. The themes and events of the Festivals formed a container not just for this shifting community who attended, but also for Damon while he was growing up. Children's ideas of the world are relatively small. Celebrating the Eight Festivals during the year helped Damon understand the annual cycles of nature and be confident in his place in ritual. He grew up with the experience that he was part of a whole community who vibrantly celebrated these Festivals.

Through those years of rituals I discovered many things. I learned how to run the rituals, successfully include children, and bring rituals to life with the participation and energy of everyone there. I also learned about the Festivals themselves, and the great Wheel they are part of. Far from becoming repetitive, I felt each time we returned to a particular Festival we went more deeply into it, and the following year more deeply again. Being in the Southern Hemisphere helped me to step beyond traditional interpretations and activities as detailed in many reference books. Each time, I tried to find what was relevant to the local natural cycle as well as current political and personal themes.

In a way Damon was my mentor. Not only was he my inspiration for creating these rituals, he was there throughout them, as he is throughout this book; invoking the God, hiding eggs for the egg hunt, leading a journey into the realms of death, or dashing into the sea on the Winter Solstice. Many stages of his growing up were lived in those rituals, and different stages of my journey as his mother. His boldness, certainty, and willingness have often taken me beyond what I felt safe or comfortable with, into the realm of living ritual. I am deeply grateful to him. This book includes memories of some of those rituals. In one of them Damon is five, in another he is nineteen, and in others he is any of the ages between. These memories are windows into what it's like for a parent and child to celebrate the Festivals together.

Moving beyond the immediately personal, the book centers on a discussion of the themes of the Festivals—not as they may have applied to people living in rural England hundreds or more years ago, but as they apply to us today. And they do apply. These Eight Festivals reflect our lives whether we live in the city or country and regardless of our spiritual tradition, age, race, belief, sexuality, or family situation. When we acknowledge and celebrate the Festivals we are honoring each part of our life: birth, growing seasons, love and letting go, harvest, and dying and death.

The Festivals have different names in different traditions and different books. It's less important what you call them, or what I've called them, and more important to know they mark points of the earth's relationship to the sun throughout the year. The solstices are the longest and shortest days of the year, and the two equinoxes have days and nights of equal length. Together the solstices and equinoxes are sometimes called the Quarter Festivals, and there's one of them every three months. The four Festivals known as the Cross-Quarter Festivals fall between the solstices and equinoxes, and their most common names are Imbolc (pronounced *Im-olc*), Beltaine, Lammas, and Samhain (most commonly pronounced *Sow-en* or *Sow-ain*). The story of these Festivals is both sequential and ongoing; the years and Festivals follow each other endlessly, in a circle or spiral known as the Wheel of the Year.

Along with many who celebrate the Wheel of the Year, I call myself a Pagan. Pagans believe that each and every one of us is a child of spirit, or divinity—of God, of Goddess—as well as a child of earth. We believe that most if not all early cultures understood and worked with the natural environments in which they lived, and that this practice was not separate from any other aspect of their lives. We also believe that in modern life, as we come close to the rhythms and realities of the land on which we live, we understand more about nature and human belonging and interaction with it. We believe we are part of the earth rather than separate from it, and in celebrating the earth's cycles we are celebrating our intimate connection to those cycles.

In marking the Eight Festivals, we begin to recognize nature and indicators of the season more clearly wherever we live, not as we imagine them but as they actually are. We come into a framework for learning the place of sunrise and sunset at different times of the year, the patterns of weather, the foliage of trees and flowers, and the seasonality of foods. We may become aware of our own yearly cycles: depression in late winter and exuberance in autumn, or whatever they may be. Eventually we become aware not just of ourselves, moving through the Wheel with the season, but of the Wheel turning through us; we learn to feel its vibrations as if it were an extension of us.

When we celebrate the Wheel of the Year, we enter into dialogue with this great force. We move through phases of observing the seasonal indicators and thus being *spoken to* and in turn *speaking to it*, as we create rituals of our own devising, commenting on what is happening. Eventually, we arrive in the realm of speaking *with it*. Just as the year turns past summer into autumn, I am in conversation with the Wheel about what it means to be in the second half of my forties; at the Winter Solstice, I am seeking ways to be inspired again; at Beltaine, I am in dialogue about our human relationships of love, lust, and fertility. We are not just observing the Wheel and being carried along with it, but we participate actively in this living system of conception, birth, growth, fullness, change, completion, death, and rebirth.

And the process is right here. The cycle of the Wheel is happening all the time, under our noses, under our feet, in our changing lives. It is available to us as soon as we raise our eyes beyond our built environment to see the sky, birds, and trees or to smell the air or eat seasonal food. Not only are our individual lives one great cycle, but so are the lives of our communities, our projects, our relationships, and our families. On this Wheel, in eight parts we can find every stage of life. Celebrating the earth's endless life eight times a year grants us opportunities to honor every aspect of our own and our children's and our community's lives. It offers an ever-available link into the living cycle of nature, of which we are inevitably a part. In celebrating the Wheel of the Year we are actively celebrating our own lives.

Perhaps in ancient times these Festivals were woven seamlessly into the fabric of people's lives. Now we have the opportunity to consciously embrace them, and in doing so we make sacred our connection to the earth and the natural cycles that govern our birth, living, and death. This book is a guide to the Eight Festivals and their relevance in contemporary life. It may inspire you to think about the cycles of life and connect more deeply with them. You can use it to help teach your children about the sacredness of life, to introduce celebrations and the different seasons, and explore related activities. You may choose to use it as a guide for creating your own

Wheel of the Year rituals, or you may prefer simply to read about the rituals as they have been in my life and my son's life. This book is designed to be a workbook, a jumping-off point, an inspiration, a challenge, and an open invitation to meet with the divine in the everyday.

How to Use This Book

Rituals of Celebration will teach you how to celebrate the natural cycle of the seasons. It includes rituals and activities for each of the Festivals as well as detailed instructions for many different aspects of ritual such as participation, altars, how to cast a circle, and various invocations. There is also a section at the end of the book on how to create your own seasonal ritual; this section only consists of guidelines, so feel free to follow your own practices and preferences if you have them. If you choose not to do a whole ritual but still want to participate in the season, a craft activity is detailed for each Festival; these are listed in the Contents pages. Most rituals contain an abbreviated form of the activity linked with that Festival.

The rituals are primarily written for those celebrating with a group, whether it is a family group, a wider social or community group, a men's or women's group, or a special interest group; however, the rituals can also be adapted for solo use. The rituals assume children will be present and sometimes include special sections for children's involvement, but the rituals will also work for adult-only groups. This book contains the basics of rituals. Much of the content is left up to you; my suggestions provide a base to begin working from, an inspiration or something to try until you feel confident creating ritual on your own.

Instructions for a ritual look very dull on a page. All the life and soul of a ritual comes in doing it; when you infuse a ritual with your own energy, creativity, song, dance, or whatever else you choose to put into a ritual, you make the ritual your own. In spite of looking dull when reduced to their basic components, rituals contain extraordinarily powerful moments. They can create deep understanding and offer revelations, both personal and general. I want this book to do more than discuss the themes of each Festival and give instructions for a ritual. I want to take you into the life of ritual, and for this reason I've included experiences of my own; for each Festival, I've written the story of what one of those rituals was like for me.

You can start celebrating the Festivals at any time of the year. I've begun with the Winter Solstice because that's at the beginning of the cycle, but the Wheel goes around and around—just as you have been traveling around and around it all your life. No time is better than another to begin—or deepen—your celebration. If you use this book as a workbook it could take you a year to travel through it. There are six to eight weeks between Festivals, providing enough time to read each new section, find its relevance to you, and prepare a ritual. You can also simply read the book from start to finish, and then put it aside and begin or continue creating your own rituals. You may also choose to just read all the memoirs or all the activities.

Different parts of the world see different types of seasons—hot and wet seasons, dry seasons, winter growth seasons, and many other variations. Wherever you are, the solstices and equinoxes still occur as the earth and sun move through a yearly cycle known as the Wheel of the Year. The Festivals of the Wheel of the Year honor and celebrate more than the seasons we experience when we plant a garden or observe the changing weather and length of the days. Humans also move through this cycle, traveling this Wheel throughout our lives as we turn from newborn babies to children, young adults to maturity, and middle age to old age, and finally reaching the point of death.

These seasons are experienced on many levels. A season of birth does not just represent seeds sprouting and the babies being born, but also whatever is beginning. This might be a new relationship, the start of a project, moving to a new home, changing jobs, or turning over a new leaf and taking a fresh approach to life. Thus at a seasonal Festival celebrating birth there may be people who have a young child, are anticipating one, or are longing for one; people who have some other new aspect to celebrate in their lives, such as a new job, a new creative project, or a new meditation practice; people who are searching for new ideas, a new relationship, or a new direction, as well as those who just come along and are reminded of and prompted toward the new.

Whether you wish to create and participate in rituals or not, the sections on the themes of each Festival will allow you to understand that Festival more deeply, and find the place where the Festivals resonate with your own life. The Wheel is cyclic and as endless as nature and so it teaches us of the most difficult-to-believe truth: life changes. If you are stuck in a long, drawn-out personal winter, reading the Winter Solstice section and then moving onto the next section may prompt your gradual turning point and emergence. If you wish you could go more deeply into your spiritual understandings, your magical practice, your self-development, or your emotional depths, try reading through the themes, memoirs, and rituals attached to the inward turn: those from Lammas through to Samhain, the darkening time of the year.

The Eight Festivals are often linked with agricultural activities such as planting and harvest, but they stand independent of these events. The four Quarter Festivals (the two equinoxes and two solstices) are astronomical events; they mark points of the earth's relationship to the sun. The solstices are the days of greatest light (Summer Solstice) and greatest dark (Winter Solstice), when the tilt of the earth has resulted in the longest or shortest possible hours of the sun reaching the earth. The two equinoxes (Spring Equinox and Autumn Equinox), occurring halfway between the solstices, have nights and days of equal length. The four remaining Festivals are known as

Cross-Quarter Festivals and they each fall roughly halfway between a solstice and an equinox.

Solstices and equinoxes happen simultaneously in both hemispheres, but while the Northern Hemisphere is experiencing Summer Solstice, the Southern Hemisphere will be experiencing Winter Solstice, and vice versa. The hemispheres simultaneously experience opposite Festivals from each other, so the Spring and Autumn Equinoxes occur on the same day, one in each hemisphere. The Southern Hemisphere celebrates Samhain (popularly known as Halloween) on the same day and night that the Northern Hemisphere celebrates Beltaine, also known as May Day. Every Festival opposites are occurring globally. You could see this pattern as a double circle, double wheel, or double spiral.

Each Festival has a wide range of variation. From place to place the experience of any Festival may be completely different—a Summer Solstice in verdant Tasmania will not resemble the same festival in the northern tropics of Darwin, just as a Hawaiian Winter Solstice will be strikingly different from a Boston one. The Festivals retain their sequencing, and thus their themes, but how those themes are played out will depend on the location. The ways that themes of birth, growth, maturity, and death play out in your life and your family's life will also be different from others, but they are the same inevitable themes following the same cycle. Celebrating this cycle brings us into living, dynamic relationship with the earth, and the cycles and seasons that mirror our own lives. The beauty and complexity of this exists when the simplicity of the Wheel is complemented by the endless variations of place, people, and rituals on any one of the Festivals.

The essential thing about the Festivals is that they are fixed calendar points marking the relationship between the earth and the sun, and therefore—because we are part of the earth—these Festivals have much to do with our relationship with the earth and the sun. Their essential relationship to each other, to the cycle of life, and what we call the Wheel of the Year remains unchanged through the centuries. However, what people did in the past to celebrate and acknowledge the Festivals is not nearly so power-ful or relevant as what we might do today and tomorrow to acknowledge and celebrate them. Our celebration will depend in part upon where we are—Southern or Northern Hemisphere, city, rainforest, coastal area, or desert. There are many books about the historic roots of these Festivals, the traditions associated with them, and the origins of their names. This book is not one of them. The rituals in this book have retained some elements of tradition in Maypoles and Lammas Dollies, but please experiment with and change these if you don't feel they belong where you are. They are symbols of the themes of one point in the cycle of life; if other symbols work better for you, discover them and use them.

The Wheel has its own medicine—it is a medicine wheel, endlessly teaching that our lives evolve and change, grow and wither, just as day and night come and go and every natural thing journeys through these same cycles. Our culture and contemporary lifestyles have encouraged us to ignore, resist, and even deny these cycles. But the Wheel is not just about cycles; it is also intrinsically about balance. Every part of the Wheel balances out every other part. Winter balances summer. Birth balances death. Joy balances grief. Planting fields balances harvesting them. Imagine a world where we were always planting and never harvesting—we would starve. Or a world always harvesting and never planting—perhaps not un-like our world today, cutting down irreplaceable rainforests, strip mining, and overfishing—eventually we will starve that way, too.

We understand that to remain forever in grief is unsustainable, although when we are grieving it seems that our grief will never end. Can we therefore understand that to remain forever in joy is also unsustainable? It would ne-cessitate denial; for sickness, death of those whom we love, and life's general difficulties occur regardless. Joy would become a forced thing, not truthful to our own experiences or feelings. When we insist on acknowledging or celebrating only parts of life, we get stuck and become out of balance. Life is a cycle. The Wheel and celebrating the Festivals of the Wheel of the Year continually teaches and reminds us how to hold the whole of the cycle, and every part of it, as sacred. When we do this we begin to experience balance not just in the world around us, but in our own lives and through the journey of our lives.

Wheel of the Year in the Northern Hemisphere

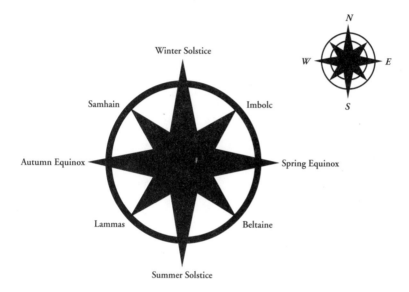

Wheel of the Year in the Southern Hemisphere

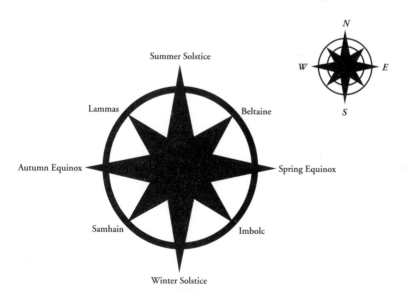

Winter Solstice

*Celebrated on or close to December 21 in the Northern Hemisphere
and June 21 in the Southern Hemisphere.*

Winter Solstice

It is cold. And dark. We gather on the beach, torches weaving back and forth as we carry supplies in from the car park and locate each other. Hushed voices, feet stamping on the sand, the remaining night stretched overhead in stars or a moon. It feels like the whole world is our circle, especially once we can discern the horizon, a line between dark sea and dark sky. The waves are subdued. Eventually someone picks up a drum. A child complains or runs up the beach; rattles are dug out of baskets and gloves are removed to start the drumming. Someone fumbles with the wood, digging a small pit in the sand to protect our fire from the wind and kindles a flame. We're here before dawn after the longest night to herald the rise of the sun and the start of the new cycle. The drummer finds a rhythm and one by one the rattles, shakers, clapping sticks, and voices join in. We stare east over the sea, wondering exactly where the sun will rise.

We've shared this morning with fishermen and surfers; a couple of times early walkers have joined us to sing songs into the predawn. We drum, rattle, and chant until we see the globe of the sun lift clear of the horizon. Every year it's startling, different, and every year beautiful. Once rain hovered all morning but didn't actually descend until the sun rose so we glimpsed it in a brief interval—rounded, brilliant, and burnt-orange sandwiched between clouds, low on the horizon, then swallowed by cloud. Once a delicate reversed rainbow of colors, violet the top of the arc, then indigo, blue, green, yellow, orange, and red the innermost color, sketched itself in long ribbons above the sea, topped with a star-like Venus. Then the sun spilled upward, achingly slowly, obliterating everything with brightness. Once it looked Egyptian: cryptic, ancient, dark-red, and impossibly powerful, the Eye of Horus born from the Underworld.

The sun takes an incredibly long time to rise. There's a whole hour of light; gathering, increasing, incrementally brighter, wider, and paler, and higher before the sun actually rises. It gets boring, so we throw ourselves into the drumming and singing. In a moment the sky's changed again, turning to lavender, lemon, yellow, peach, rose-blushed, and if there are clouds low down there can be sparks of brilliance tugging at our eyes. We direct our voices, our intent, our beating and calling over this way, that way—is that it? Is that it? Finally, when it really rises there can be no doubt at all; it is liquid, molten gold, more intense than anything we imagined, more definitely a globe than we were led to believe, with all those colors bleeding everywhere. Each second it rises higher, pulling itself over the line of horizon, or we slide toward it, the earth tilting like a lover as it brightens and lightens and begins taking on its piercing, daytime costume; though for a moment we saw it unclothed, just for a few blinks.

When the lower rim of the sun clears the horizon we strip off our clothes, balancing foot to foot on the cold sand and head toward the sea, some eagerly and some in huge resistance, shouting and dodging waves or diving sleekly under. My son Damon races to be first in every time, when he's eight and when he's eighteen and all the years between. Naked and tearing down the sand, shouting out a challenge to other children and slower adults, still battling with socks, underclothes, and reluctance.

Every year the sea is warmer than we expect. It's beautiful: the froth of waves, the cleanness of it, the exhilaration and looking around at bodies half-submerged, playing in the elements, a line of naked women holding hands or a man body-surfing or children shrieking at waves. Eventually we haul ourselves out; by now there are others arriving at our beach, uncertain about this avalanche of naked bodies. The sand is cold and we huddle around the fire, dripping, sharing towels and trying to get our clothes on. Sometimes we've cooked breakfast on that fire and opened thermoses of hot tea, or we've gone to a café, open early for surfers and dog walkers, and we're always slightly high on the sun rising, the ocean dip, the new year.

Once we saw a whale, not far out at all, in the predawn light. One time a pelican flew low overhead and then cornered, turned and landed nearby, waddling up toward us as if enquiring about our gathering. Damon walked to meet it and we've got a photo that looks like they're having a conversation. There are sea eagles too, in the dawn updrafts. It's the start of the year, the base point of our Wheel, and I'm amazed we don't do this every day, and grateful we do it at least once a year.

Winter Solstice Memoir

The house is cold and we haven't lit a fire. People remark on it as they come through the door, and again when they enter the cavernous living space. They keep their coats on, crossing to the fireplace hopefully as we wait to begin the ritual. It's late afternoon, still light for another hour, but we've timed it so darkness will gradually fall over us. I feel edgy; we're experimenting in this ritual and I don't really know if it will work.

We cast a circle with eight of us standing in the compass points at the extreme perimeters of the house, each making a low, continuous sound. We start with Imbolc, southeast in the Southern Hemisphere, and work around the circle; Spring Equinox, Beltaine, Summer Solstice, Lammas, Autumn Equinox, Samhain, and Winter Solstice. Each tone is particular to its direction, and I fall in love with each one of those voices, unseen from my Summer Solstice place in the kitchen. As each one chimes in, overlaying the sound with a new note, the song builds and strengthens. We don't use words at all. We kneel together to acknowledge Below and then stand. We turn to face the center, strengthening our sound, and gradually walk inward. My point is the exact opposite of the Winter Solstice Festival we're celebrating; holding the point associated with Winter Solstice is a close friend. I've worked magic with her for many years. I find her voice in the soundscape and we sing together.

My house—a tall, hexagonal, split-block structure—holds and amplifies the energy, and I can feel my connections to the others casting the circle like visible threads, vibrating and weaving closer and closer as we walk inward. It feels as though we are shaping the first ever circle, the beginning of the universe, carving it out of sound and space. Our voices vibrate and I imagine planets finding their courses around the sun, harmonizing and differentiating but all working together to create this whole magnificent thing, a circle made of liquid sounds, the very air around us cooperating as we move into alignment with one another. My place beckons to me, known and loved and also revelatory—this place! Here! At the pinnacle of the circle; sublime, utter, and unique yet simply one identical segment of this structure.

When we reach the cluster of people who've come to the ritual, we take their hands, stepping into a loose circle with them and still sounding. We raise our linked hands into the air, the tone shifting as we join those eight resonances together and call in a final note to Above. Then we drop our hands, let go, and fall silent.

Into the center of the circle I step. I speak for the Goddess and feel her fill me, dark night and belly rounded with the promise of birth. I breathe deep, remembering that heavy dragging pull, that grinding against the pelvic bones, the nauseous and terrifying trembling of flesh as it rearranged itself. I gasp with the eagerness and ferocity of labor. I'm on the edge of tears and my voice shakes; the words almost sing themselves out of my mouth. *I am the mother! I am the Star Goddess, Earth Goddess, Great Mother; my body carries the new. On this night, the Winter Solstice, I give birth! Forth from my womb, I bring him!*

I crouch down, squat with my head bent as a man steps forward, prowling the center. He's dressed in gold and he speaks like a lover, blazing, of the relationship between the earth and sun, how far away we'd turned from him and now we were coming back, unfolding our secrets again. He lowers his voice to speak of this night, the changing point, as if it were too dear to him to do more than whisper of it, even in sacred space. Then he melts back into the circle.

Another man, wearing black, steps forward and calls out, *The old king is dead, the old Gods are dead. It is time, time, time for the new!* and he flings his arms up as if he himself was the one who had died, his voice tearing as it rips apart with the ending of the old world. Then Damon steps into the center. He happens to be the only child here, and he meets the eyes of those around him, signaling that he will carry that promise, that hope into the future. He's ten and he speaks in the clear, carrying voice used for proclaiming prophesy, by bell ringers in the streets or oracles of the ancient pantheons. *Tonight is the birth of a new child.*

One by one the people there speak of what the Winter Solstice means to them. They are variously nervous, confident, loud, uncertain, and brief, and all of them are still cold, shifting from foot to foot, crossing their arms and waiting for it to get warmer.

Each person has brought a colored candle. With a collection of glitter, ribbons, essential oils, tiny stickers, and sharp knives for inscribing, we carve and decorate our candles to express our wishes, hopes, and dreams for the year that will be birthed tonight. There are red candles for passion and green for prosperity and growth, there are white candles for peace and silver for magic. It continues to get darker and we don't turn on the lights. My yellow candle has hearts carved into it for love and a spiraled silver thread for happiness. We make candleholders from twists of cardboard, then tuck our candles away for later.

What I vividly remember, all these years later, is the men's piece of the ritual. Dusk was falling and we were getting colder as they danced toward us. They formed an outer ring around the women, gazing deep into our eyes as they passed by each of us. They moved slowly and deliberately, and I felt we were being paced around by lions, admiring predators. But I felt animal as well in the growing dark, feeling their eyes acknowledging, honoring. Then suddenly they whirled into a dance, stamping and shouting. Each of them grabbed a woman's hands, swirling around chaotically so that each pair became a whirling galaxy of its own, centered on the gravity of their eyes, a dance before they let go and dashed into the center, huddling together and toning, loud and deep and strong, their heads bent over, hands busy.

I had no idea what they were doing; it was a part of the ritual I hadn't written and couldn't predict, so I was caught up in the moment of it, not trying to second-guess or contain it. They were charged and they fiercely came together, with great purpose. I felt caught up in someone else's spell that was magnificent, beyond my dreams, and ordered by a mind other than my own. That mind was set in its course and absolute, immense. The toning reached a climax and they punched all their hands up in the air and turned outward, all at once, throwing great handfuls of glitter up and over us and themselves. The dying light caught in glints and glimmers, flickering and drifting down like snowflakes, like magic dust, like wishes or seeds that had been nurtured in the dark earth.

We were caught in it, stilled and silenced. It descended, covering us, decorating everything. They had pocketed the glitter from the candle decorating and then charged it with their chanting, a kind of group insemination so raw I was speechless, amazed with its beauty and power. We all glittered, all night; it was in our hair and on our clothes and skin. I spent months vacuuming it out of the rugs. Even if anyone doubted that the sun would be born again that night they couldn't doubt the energy of those men, their fierce celebration of the life force, their honoring of the feminine and willingness to give to the turning of the Wheel.

It was really dark by now; we could barely see and so we launched into the chaos segment, the unformed space between the end of the old year and the beginning of the new. There was wild energy everywhere, the circle had been cast through the whole house and every corner resonated in jarring, shouted, spilled chaos. In the dark we screamed and shouted, ridding ourselves of the old, stamping and flinging ourselves about, and rattling chaotically and drumming madly and discordantly and on and on and on out into the darkness until each one of us collapsed from exhaustion, drained, with nothing left.

I screamed along with the rest; my unmet longings, my loneliness and fear of being alone forever, my distress at the relationship I'd lost, years ago now but I couldn't seem to get over it. I screamed out my overwhelm at being alone with a child in a huge house on an unkempt piece of land and for wanting more, much more, in my life than this. I rattled and shouted and whirled until I was dizzy. Yet I stayed alert; I stayed aware of the shape of the ritual, the placement of people, and the level of noise and energy—not like in the men's game, when I was lost to it, swept up in the magic they'd created.

Finally we were silent; squatting, sitting, or lying on the floor, not a drumbeat left between us, nothing but ragged breath and a deep sigh here or there. The stillness settled in the dark and we entered the eye of the Winter Solstice, the nothing place. The birthing place. The floor in my house is concrete and I happened to be on a piece of it that wasn't covered by a rug. It was dark, the floor was hard, it was still cold, it was silent. Night had come. We were in the pitch of the year.

And then, into the stillness and quiet, a word dropped. A sequence of words, a man's voice dripping liquid sounds into our dark night; serpent voice, sinuous with melting phrases. My bedroom, on the second floor, has a window overlooking where we were flung about on the floor. I had seen earlier that he headed up there, at the start of our chaos; and he, a poet and singer, spoke these words unseen, out into the long darkness.

The land forms itself. Out of chaos it is born, out of darkness.

Each word pulled itself, almost, from the air and coalesced in the surrounds of space before floating down to us.

There is a serpent formed from rainbows; she twists her way across the land. She creates the hills, the rivers and the secret waterways. Mountains are left behind her, valleys and fertile plains.

He is singing the world into being, out the other side of night, into the dawn. He tells of the dawn of the land. We are back at the beginning of things.

The people are born in her tracks; the tree people, the animal people, all the different tribes. The children are born, one by one.

I remember that I am the Goddess, that I am giving birth tonight.

The sun rises. Out of the darkness comes golden light, warmth across the land.

The Wheel turns. It turns through me. I am rebirthing myself; my own hope and my wishes not to be alone are surely met this night, in that great sounding at the beginning of the ritual, by the men's game, by the people here. At the moment of greatest darkness will come the light, reborn always and always. I am alone on the floor in the darkness of my house, yet poetry slides through the night, my skin is glittered with promise and everywhere around me I hear breathing—others also waiting to be reborn. No longer exhausted and collapsed, but now expectant, alert in the still dark.

Damon is crouched a few meters away, near the center of the room. He makes small rustling and scraping sounds with his box of matches. A flame flares as he lights his candle; the one he decorated earlier, with colored wax dripped all over it, stickers and ribbons and wishes wound around it. He holds the candle up and doesn't need any words. We fumble around in the mostly dark room, finding our candles and bringing them to Damon. One by one we light our candles from his. The light, born in a cluster at the center, spreads through the room like little stars in the dark, vast space. Someone brings a flame over to the fireplace and finally the fire is lit.

We gather back into a circle as the fire roars behind us. We sing full of cheer, holding our candles up and releasing their wishes into the new year. As the chant dies down, the eight of us who cast the circle begin sounding again for the eight directions, eight different tones blending together and we raise our arms high, acknowledging Above. Then we turn and walk, still sounding, slowly out to the perimeters of the house. When I get to my place I turn back to see as much as I can, those little candles marking the bigness of our circle. We drop to the ground, bringing the sound low but still loud, resonating into the floor and thanking Below. Then we blow out our candles and fall silent, releasing the circle.

The Light Struck in the Dark

The beginning of things. Birth. Birth in the darkness. Born from darkness we arrive into light.

In the beginning there was nothing—and then everything, an explosion, light and energy expanding everywhere. Impossibly, the universe is born.

The seed lies silent in the dark earth of winter. Unobserved, it sprouts and sends out roots, seeking nourishment. The seed sends out one tentacle, questing, above. Seeking light. It pierces green through the soil's crust into light. Becoming.

The days grow colder, shorter. Sap slows down, leaves fall from the trees, animals seek shelter, birds depart. The sun stays more briefly and retreats earlier; night extends her grip. Later and later the sun rises and earlier it sets until it reaches its furthest place toward the earth's pole, and almost unbelievably, the next morning starts back. The year is born again.

The Goddess labors through the dark night. A child is born to her, a son. She gives birth in the Underworld, at midnight, or at dawn. The birth of her child is marked by the sun-that-is-star symbolizing growth, warmth, and life. His is the birth of light. There is rejoicing, celebration for this Year God who will grow to become child, lover, king, and sacrifice in turn, succumbing to the earth's embrace and awaiting rebirth.

A child is born to the Goddess Ishtar, or reborn to the Celtic Cerridwen, or born of the earth mother, or Isis, in a thousand myths and stories.

A child is born to a woman in a stable. His birth is marked by a star in the heavens. Each year his birth is remembered, for his life brings light to the people.

A child is born in a hospital, in a tent, a hut, or a field. A child is born in a slum, in a palace, in a suburb, city, or town. A child is born on a farm, in war, in peace, into a democracy, into a military dictatorship, in a refugee camp. A child is born in a commune, in a family, to a single mother. A child is born to black, white, Asian, indigenous, or mixed-race parents. A child is born male, female, privileged, wealthy, poor, healthy, damaged, weak, wanted, unwanted, first born, eighth born, premature, full term, by caesarean, after long labor, or easily. A child is born. This is new life, inexplicable, miraculous, and *new each time*. This is the light struck in the dark. All wonder, all potential; a life brought forth out of the darkness of infinite time, from the earth, from a woman's body, from the unimaginable before.

The child is new, the child is one of us. Each one carrying the light within. Each one born out of darkness. This is the beginning place—birth. The mystery brought forth, revealed again and again. And not just with humans. With animals, trees, birds, reptiles, and insects, life becomes. Life is. Each life is part of the web, the complex dance of life, of the earth and sun. Each child carries that spark of the earthly marriage with the divine, of divinity itself. That moment when the cells join and then start to divide, isn't that a miracle? The same kind of miracle that results in the birth of a star, or the beginning of the universe itself?

The beginning is shrouded in darkness. The unborn bird inside its egg, the seed in the earth, the child forming in the womb—all in darkness. Beginnings remain mysterious, however closely we plot them or however much planning goes into them. Birth and transformation are not dependent on outside factors but have their own internal programs, remaining essentially uncontrolled. The process of birth is coded into our bodies—our own and our mothers'. It is not a process we have to understand to have it happen. Although it can be *overwritten* in individual instances (with induced births or caesareans, for example) it cannot be *rewritten*; the next generation reverts to the original encoded pattern. As for transformation, we can tempt ourselves toward that state, offer our bodies and minds circumstances we think may trigger it such as initiation, therapy, retreats, or spiritual discipline. Yet we cannot order it or guarantee it. Each of us has at least several times of transformation or rebirth over a lifetime.

This birth and rebirth is the theme of the Winter Solstice, yet the process that results in the symbolic birth of the year, this new beginning, is given little attention. The process is played out through the previous few months of the solar year. It is the preparation for the new that occurs in the part of the cycle dedicated to the dying and stripping away of external and material things, a process of whittling down. It includes a time of utter darkness even if it is only the length of the longest night. In spiritual or psychological terms, this is the dark night of the soul.

We have a basic understanding of this as long as it concerns the moon or the Winter Solstice. When it comes to our own lives, we are not usually so forgiving. We structure our lives to contain an endless line of successes, an onward-and-upward totalitarian theme. We do not encourage or often even allow for regular periods of stripping away, of letting go, of becoming less and less—not in our work, our relationships, or our activities. If there has been a loss, we do not allow time for natural turnarounds to occur. Instead we force them as if they were greenhouse plants. Grief, for example, is unavoidable, but it's desired by all that the grieving one get through it as quickly as possible. We require grieving people to act as though they are no longer in grief within a short time after a loss. The long gradual and natural process of letting go, of a free-fall into the dark and the unknown, is terrifying to us.

The Winter Solstice is the nadir, or lowest point, on the Wheel of the Year. Through the preceding six months everything has completed, died, and been released until hope and light are born again in deepest winter. Light is not born from light, but out of darkness. It is precisely at this darkest, coldest point that light is celebrated—not because it is strongest then, but because of its promise. A candle flame is a tiny thing in a dark night, but it is what our eyes focus on. It is not greater than the dark that surrounds it, but by its contrast the light defies its size.

Perhaps to our detriment, for it is only half the equation, it is light we inarguably worship. The Winter Solstice celebrates the return of light and the birth of the year and that's the moment our joy, relief, and celebration of light erupt. Light equates to life for us, at a primeval level; so even though it's unfair that *both* solstices are dedicated to celebrating light—the return of the sun at the Winter Solstice and the full strength of the sun at the Summer Solstice—that's how it is. Just as we turn on artificial lights when it's dark or minimize any downtime in our lives (time devoted merely to dreaming, musing, drifting, or personal or spiritual exploration) so in our rituals and our lives we often attempt to ignore and minimize the dark.

Minimizing darkness is only effective up to a point. We are creatures of night as well as the day. We need sleep to survive, and some of the things that occur during sleep—growth, healing, dreaming, and rest—cannot occur properly when we are awake. Dreams, those mysterious other lives we lead when we sleep, may inspire problem solving, warnings, new directions, and understanding. As well as dreaming, night is a time for intimacy, relaxation, sharing stories, music, and dance. The dark is a place of mysteries, of initiation, even of love. The Winter Solstice contains several of these threads vital to our well-being.

When we think about birth, whether it is the birth of a person, project, or a year, we realize we cannot arrive at it immediately. Birth entails a conception, pregnancy, and labor. Even a project, new business, or a relationship must go through a process prior to coming to life, including inspiration, focus, choice (and sometimes sacrifice), trust, and hard work. A woman in labor releases whomever she was prior to the birth to literally be reborn into a new identity with the birth of her baby. A new start in life, whether a change of career, a new relationship, or a spiritual commitment involves labor, releasing the old, and a full-hearted investment in the new.

New things are scary as well as positive and enticing. You can't have the new without letting go of the old. The year could not be born again if it had not died. A new relationship cannot be successful when we still cling to an old one. A new project demands we be present and focused in our attention and energy. To step out of the known into the unknown is something we all do with each new job, love, project, child, or adventure we undertake. Some of us structure our lives to minimize the new as much as possible. We create safe—although perhaps static—jobs, houses, marriages, and relationships and shore ourselves up against change, preferring what is known and safe to the risk of the new.

Yet each of us has the experience of transformative change. We go through times in our lives of apparently losing everything or nearly everything we rely on and care about. Somehow in the very deepest part of it we experience a revelation, an epiphany, and a return to our essential selves. A rebirth. This leads us to recreate our relationship to our own lives and ourselves so profoundly that afterward we feel almost like a different person. We are not strangers to ourselves, but rather deeply recognizable. It seems that before we were living in some outer shell of our personality, and now we have been reborn we are far more true to ourselves, living our real lives.

The ongoing story of life and death—the story of success, stability, or stasis followed by change, upheaval, loss, and eventually transformation—is a story happening all around us, irrelevant to our will and implacable. We can even watch it monthly in the heavens as the moon begins lessening progressively, immediately after its fullest phase, until it disappears entirely. After a few nights it reappears in a different part of the sky and in reverse to what it looked like before. We can watch it on the solar level as the days get shorter and shorter, the sun rising later and later and staying risen for shorter periods, closer to the horizon until the nadir is reached and everything reverses back.

The yearly advent of the Winter Solstice reminds us that living is the cycle of growth and change and that regularly we must strip everything away. It reminds us to celebrate the new when it arrives. Denial or resistance to this pattern doesn't prevent new things from occurring; perhaps unexpected and unwelcome things are even more noticeable when a person tries to create a life that is unchanging. Denial and resistance make us rusty and unpracticed in our acceptance of the new, creating resentment and limiting or undermining the effects of rebirth.

Yet there is this wonder. The light struck in the dark. The stars in the night sky. Sunrise. New leaves budding on the trees. A new star. A bird hatching from an egg; a field greened with sprouts. A child born.

Winter Solstice Ritual

Notes: "Ritual Basics" on page 295 covers many aspects of ritual, including grounding, casting circles, invocations, and participation.

How to make Winter Solstice Wishing Candles is described in more detail on page 47.

If you have children present, you may choose to moderate or eliminate part of section 7, "Naming Fears".

Section 8, "The Voice in the Darkness and the First Light" is the central part of this ritual.

Ask everyone to bring:
- A dinner candle in a color representing their intent for the coming year (for example, green for growth, white for peace, or red for passion) and a candleholder

- A rattle, drum, or other noise-maker

- Food for the Winter Solstice Feast if you are going to have one

Other things needed for this ritual:

- A fire, laid but not lit. This can be an outside fire, an indoor fire in a fireplace, a symbolic fire in a cauldron, or if none of those are possible, a new white pillar candle

- Candle ends of many colors (crayons work as well)

- Carving implements (small sharp knives or house nails will do)

- Small stickers and tiny objects (shells, charms, or seeds) that can be stuck onto candles

- A few different essential oils

- Narrow ribbons or colored thread

- Glitter or glitter glue

- Newspaper or cardboard to cover the work surface

- A central candle and lighter or matches

Clothing suggestion:

- Each person to wear either all white or all black—if you give this choice, you will probably end up with a mix of all white and all black, which is ideal

Roles in ritual:

These can be done by different people or one or two people can take all or most of the roles, depending on how confident and experienced the group is:

- Casting the circle and calling directions, which can be done by several different people or all by one person

- Invocations, done by two people (can be the same people who called the directions)

- Grounding

- Leading warm-ups

- Leading discussion and giving instructions

- The voice in the darkness

- Someone to light the first candle (it's nice to have a child do this)

- Timekeeper (this may not be necessary, or can be combined with another role)

- Drummer/song leader

Length of Ritual: 1.5 hours

Ritual

1. Gathering

Welcome the group to the ritual space and take care of any housekeeping. If some people are unfamiliar with ritual etiquette, briefly explain how you'd like the ritual to run.

Announce the intention of the ritual. For example: *Tonight we celebrate the longest night and the moment the light is born again*, *The intention of this ritual is to honor the Winter Solstice*, or *We come together to honor the Earth Goddess and the new-born sun.*

Ask everyone to introduce themselves briefly. Start with yourself, giving a demonstration of the type of introduction you want. If you have a large group (more than twenty), you can ask people simply to introduce themselves to the person or people next to them.

2. Grounding and Warm-ups

Warm-ups are optional, but are great in a group that doesn't know each other well or isn't practiced in ritual, and also in groups with children.

GROUNDING:

- Briefly introduce the idea of grounding. Grounding is done to help everyone to become fully present, feel alive in their bodies, and release any distractions.

- Offer a seasonal grounding using the imagery of birth—the birth of an animal, bird, human, or star.

- Speak slowly and clearly, adding varying intonations to your voice as the grounding moves through its different stages.

- Finish with a clear instruction for everyone to open their eyes (if they were shut) and become fully present.

SUGGESTED WARM-UPS:

- **Physical:** Body shaping; have someone speak the name of an object and have everyone shape their bodies to become that thing. You can begin with objects such as a flower and an ant and move on to more complex things that take several people or the whole group to create, such as a castle, a forest, a dark and stormy night.

- **Vocal:** Soundscape; begin with a few practice sounds, then ask everyone to close their eyes and create a group soundscape, imagining the beginning of the universe. Continue for a few minutes.

3. Creating a Sacred Space

- **Cast a circle:** If you want to give your circle casting a particularly Winter Solstice flavor, this can be done by placing tea lights around the perimeter of your circle and having the caster light them as they cast the circle. Otherwise, have someone walk around the perimeter of your circle drawing the outline of the circle with their hand or a magical tool.

- **Call to the directions and the elements:** Have four people
  each call to one direction and element and then all together
  call to Above and Below. If you prefer, this can also be done
  by pairs of people in each direction or all by one person.

Northern Hemisphere:

East	Air	New light, the dawn
South	Fire	Promise of light and warmth
West	Water	Past, all that has happened
North	Earth	Darkness, the longest night
Above and Below		

Southern Hemisphere:

East	Air	New light, the dawn
North	Fire	Promise of light and warmth
West	Water	Past, all that has happened
South	Earth	Darkness, the longest night
Above and Below		

- **Invocations:** A woman invokes the Earth Goddess. A child
  or a man invokes the birth of the Summer Lord, the Year
  King, or the sun.

4. Introducing the Winter Solstice

Have one person stand forward and talk about the Winter Solstice. Include
the information that this is midwinter, the longest night, and after this the
days start to lengthen. Explain that even though it is the darkest point of
the whole year, the birth of light is celebrated and new beginnings arise when
the old is finished. The Year King (the sun) is seen as being born on this night.

You might also like to include local information. For example, if you
live somewhere where the timing of the winter sunrise is drastically different than that of the summer sunrise, you can talk about the effect this has.

After the initial explanation, ask each person to contribute their own ideas about what the Winter Solstice means or about what this time of the year means to them. It may mean holidays, or a time of cold and darkness, or of quiet. It may represent the New Year when people will be making resolutions and plans. If it is a large group (over twenty people) you can break into smaller groups for this section.

You may wish to include a discussion of Christmas symbolism, and how many traditional Pagan symbols and elements are included in contemporary Christmas celebrations, such as the evergreen tree, candles, and the birth of a child who represents the God.

The Winter Solstice also symbolizes a birth or a spark of the new. This may correspond to something in people's lives, such as the literal birth of a child, a pregnancy, the beginning of a relationship, a new career, or other aspect of newness in their lives. Discussing these life issues will bring the themes of the Winter Solstice closer to home than abstract discussions of snow and long nights (particularly if you are not in the Northern Hemisphere). This can be done in a second round of sharing and will make the ritual much more immediate and relevant.

5. Learning the Chant

Introduce the chant or chants you will be using later in the ritual. There are many chants on CDs, online, and in songbooks. You may already have favorite chants that are well known to your group. You might also have a songwriter among you. Choose a simple song or chant that is true to the themes of your ritual and teach it to the group by singing it a couple of times and then teaching it line by line. It's useful to sing it through together at least eight or ten times, so when you begin singing later in the ritual everyone can easily join in without being having to be reminded of the words or tune.

6. Making Winter Solstice Wishing Candles

This activity is described in detail on page 47, immediately following the ritual.

Explain that everyone is going to make a Winter Solstice candle to reflect their intentions, hopes, and wishes for the coming year. The intentions will be released as the candle burns down.

The steps for making the candles are:

• Set the intent.

• Carve shapes, symbols, or words into the candle.

• Drip colored wax or melted crayon onto the candle, each color representing a different quality (for example, use red for passion, white for peace, or silver for magic).

• You can add stickers or tiny objects to your candle to further represent your wishes (stick them on with a drop of melted wax).

• Add a few drops of an essential oil to support the intention (for example, lavender for healing, rose for love, or jasmine for sweetness).

• Add a binding ribbon or thread at the base if you wish.

The candles will be used later in the ritual. Place them in their candle-holders on or near the altar.

7. Naming Fears and the Night of Chaos

You may have timed your ritual for dusk, or it may already be dark. You should turn the lights out as the next parts of this ritual are done in darkness. You may go outside, in which case you should take your drums, rattles, the Winter Solstice candles, and a source of fire (a lighter or matches) with you.

Explain what will happen in the next two parts of the ritual (Naming Fears and the Night of Chaos) and that there will not be a break between them. Make it clear that no one should leave the gathering at this point; if anyone feels uncomfortable, that individual should move to the side and wait for the section to finish. Remind everyone you are in a sacred circle and are walking together into the longest night. Give clear instructions for the Night of Chaos. The gap between the old and the new year is the time for chaos to come forth, and you will all represent this with your rattles, drums, voices, and wild movements. When each person feels they have expressed it as fully as they can and there is no more left inside them, they should sit or lie down.

Start by standing or sitting in a circle. Talk a little about the longest night, and what that may have been like for our distant ancestors. Make a parallel with our lives today; maybe your longest night was a night you spent sitting by a beloved parent, friend, or child. Perhaps your longest night was a period of depression or severe illness, the ending to a relationship, or a feeling of failure. Ask people to remember their own longest nights. If there are children present, you can moderate this part of the ritual, but children have fears and difficulties like everyone else and are often quite willing to share them.

Begin the Naming Fears yourself and go around the circle two or three times. This encourages people who might not speak otherwise. Anyone can pass if they don't wish to name a fear. Fears could be things like *I'm afraid of dying, I'm afraid I won't be good at this job, I'm afraid of spiders*, or *I'm afraid I won't ever have a child*. In your explanation make it clear these fears should be named but not explained, and each sentence should begin with the words *I'm afraid*.

Monitor the energy people have on speaking these fears and decide whether to go around the circle only twice, or a third time. Alternatively, at the end of the second round you can ask everyone to shout out any remaining fears all at once (lead this yourself). You can shout the same fear two or three times, just to keep the noise going for half a minute or so. This shouting is a good transition into the Night of Chaos.

Break into chaotic drumming or rattling for the Night of Chaos. If others don't follow, immediately call out to remind them that *now is the Night of Chaos!* and keep going. Dance or fling your body about, pouring energy into your voice and your noise-making. Shout, cry, and scream; imagine yourself giving voice to the great chaos of the universe, which also abides within us. Encourage a full expression, keeping an eye on anyone who seems especially distressed or uncomfortable. If you have a large group (more than twenty) you may wish to designate one or two people to remain aware of all the others.

This process should last for about five minutes. When it dies down, allow complete silence to fall and extend.

8. The Voice in the Darkness and the First Light

After a silence of several minutes, the speaker begins. Use an inspirational passage, myth, song, or poem, whether written by yourselves or another. The speaker should either have memorized the words or improvise, as it will be completely dark.

When the silence falls again (it will be a very different type of silence), the First Light (a candle in the center) is lit. It's lovely to have a child do this.

Still in silence, show people by example it's time to get up, find their Winter Solstice candle, and bring it forward to light it from the First Light.

9. Raising Energy

Once the candles are lit, quietly begin the song. If you have prepared a fire, light it now. Let people come together and allow the song to gather strength, focus, and volume.

Split the song into a round if you wish. You can move about the space singing, holding your candles, and looking into each other's eyes; you may simply remain in a circle. You can invoke the energy of fire or the sun to ignite your wishes and intentions.

Bring the song up to full strength and raise energy at this point, if you wish. Bring the song to a strong close, leading with the drum.

10. Complete the Ritual

Honor and thank those invoked, acknowledge the directions and elements in the reverse order that they were called, and dissolve the circle. Usually the same people who did the invoking, casting, and calling do these steps.

- **Acknowledge:** The sun (the Summer Lord or Year King) is acknowledged and thanked by a child or a man. The Earth Goddess is acknowledged and thanked by a woman.

- **Acknowledge the directions and elements:**

  Northern Hemisphere:
  Below and Above

North	Earth	Longest night
West	Water	Past
South	Fire	Coming light and warmth
East	Air	Rising sun, dawn

  Southern Hemisphere:
  Below and Above

South	Earth	Longest night
West	Water	Past
North	Fire	Coming light and warmth
Eas	Air	Rising sun, dawn

- **Dissolve the circle:** If a circle was cast, the same person walks around it in the opposite direction, gathering up the energy or otherwise dispersing it. If tea lights are still lit around the edges of the circle, put them out now.

Thank each person for coming and for what they have contributed. Begin your Winter Solstice Feast, if you are having one.

Winter Solstice Activity: Wishing Candles

You can make Winter Solstice Wishing Candles as part of a larger ritual or it can be your whole ritual. Children love making these candles and lighting them on the longest night of the year. This is a gentle introduction to magic and the Wheel of the Year, with an opportunity to talk with each child about what they wish for and how their hopes and wishes might be represented by the candle and its decorations. Of course, you can make the candle by yourself or with friends.

Wishing Candles work with the element of fire and you can explore your relationship with fire while making and burning the candle.

I buy colored candles for this, but you could make your own. You can roll candles from beeswax sheets, or use a dipping method with molten wax or create a mold and pour your candle. These last two methods allow you to layer different colors of wax. When working with hot wax, be careful and supervise children very closely.

You will need:

- One dinner-style candle per person (in a variety of colors)

- Other ends of different-colored candles, small pieces of colored wax, or crayons

- Pen-knife or similar carving instrument (a house nail works well)

- Tokens such as very small feathers, crystals, shells, sequins, stickers, or small coins

- Essential oils relevant to your intention (for example, lavender for healing)

- Glitter, narrow ribbons, or thread

- Newspaper to protect your working surface

- One candleholder per candle

Time:

- 30 minutes to create your Wishing Candle, longer if you are actually making candles

Intention

Before setting the intention you may like to invoke the powers of fire, of light in the darkness, and of rebirth. Then ask each person what wishes and hopes they would like to set into their candle. People may choose things such as a new job, health, love, financial security, or inner peace. Children often choose things like finding a friend, feeling more confident at school, or solving a problem. Once everyone is clear on their purpose, everyone should choose a candle of a color that represents the nature of their wish. For example, you might choose white for a new beginning, red for love, green for something you wish to grow, or blue for peace of mind.

An example of a finished candle for joy might be yellow with flowers and suns carved into it, pink and gold wax droplets on its surface, scented with citrus oil, and bound at the bottom with a gold thread.

Method

Either explain the whole activity at the beginning and then leave each person to make their own way through it, or explain in stages (listed below) and keep the group together through the process. This is a messy activity, so spread newspaper beneath you. Candles are a fire hazard, and hot wax can be painful, so be very aware of naked flames and make sure there's enough space for everyone to work easily.

- Introduce the theme of the Winter Solstice and explain that Wishing Candles have your wishes and hopes for the new year set into them. When the candle is lit and burns (which could be in a ceremony following the candle-making), the wishes and hopes are released. The light of the candle's flame represents the light of the Winter Solstice, the return of light and warmth to the earth. You can use these candles to bring in bright hopes for your future and release your wishes into the new year.

- With children, discuss what they want and come back to them at the different stages to check they have a clear idea of what to do.

- Using a sharp object (knife, nail, or another tool) inscribe something on the candle, such as hearts or a single word.

- Choose three to five qualities you think will assist in making your spell work; for example, calm, inspiration, open heart, and forgiveness. For each quality, choose one color from your available supply of other candles or colored crayons; the color should correspond with one of your chosen qualities. One at a time, light the candles and drip their colored wax onto your Wishing Candle (or melt a few drops of the crayon), concentrating on the quality you wish to invoke while you do this. You can run the drips along the length of the candle, or around the candle or just put them in dots. If you have carved shapes in your candle, you can fill them with wax of another color.

- Now choose some tokens or stickers to represent your intention. Use wax to stick the tokens onto your candle.

- Choose one or more essential oils to drip or smear onto your candle, depending on the desired outcome. You might choose something a little unusual, such as eucalyptus for cleansing or olive oil for riches.

- Add glitter if you wish, or bind a colored thread or ribbon around the base of your candle.

- When the candles are finished, have everyone revisit their intention. You can then light the candles from a central flame and set them to burn on an altar or each person can take theirs home to burn at an appropriate time. Ideally you would light the candles on the eve of the Winter Solstice.

- Please remember all candles are a serious fire hazard, and you need to stay with your candle the entire time it is alight. Use the time for an activity related to your wishes.

Imbolc

*Celebrated on February 2 in the Northern Hemisphere
and August 2 in the Southern Hemisphere.*

Imbolc

At Imbolc (pronounced *Im-olc*) I'm drawn to very simple rituals, such as writing blessings on ribbons, tying wishes into trees, planting seeds, and speaking poetry. I have a memory of an Imbolc in an orchard with a few men and women and some children. It was sunny but still cold; we wore sweaters and scarves. The earth was wet under our boots. Damon was about six and he played the young God; we chose a little girl, about four, to be the Goddess. Toward the end of the ritual, the men lifted Damon high in their arms, and he sprinkled handfuls of blossom over the little girl while she looked up and laughed. That's Imbolc for me, small communities gathering together and celebrating, seeing life unfold again in the blossom on the fruit trees and children playing together.

To celebrate Imbolc is to engage in trust. Traditionally, people would have had to trust they would be given another year of subsistence farming; that pregnancies and births would go well and crops would flourish so there would be enough food. This is a time of year when everything's uncertain. The people of the past would have thrown themselves wholeheartedly into another spring and summer with no guarantees of harvest or success. A modern equivalent might be to ask ourselves, *Do we trust that our newborn babies will be fine, that they will transition safely through school, family life, friends, and adolescence to adulthood? Do we trust a new relationship to be supportive and joyful, a new job to go well, or our inspiration to bear fruit?* At Imbolc we are asked to trust almost before anything has happened to justify that trust.

It seems that our world is becoming an increasingly difficult place to trust. Relationships and families split and scatter and there is an overwhelming emphasis on self-reliance rather than interdependence. People come and go in our lives, even those we believe should be permanent fixtures. Almost no one has a job for life. Massive infrastructure like the international economy—and even the climate—can't be relied on. Our food has toxins, our mobile phones give us cancer, and our governments show little apparent interest in caretaking and solving problems that nearly everyone on the planet wants to fix (a lack of clean drinking water for a significant part of the world's population, for example). Even religion—a permanent and inarguable structure in most earlier cultures—is no longer a strong force in Western culture, and established religions are experiencing political and moral crises as well as falling numbers.

For all its apparent lack of complexity, Imbolc carries the mystery of the unknown. It is near the start of the cycle. It may symbolize the promising beginning of something new—a relationship, garden, family, creative project, or business—but it is still unknown how these new things will develop. The developments of these new things are in the lap of the Gods; not even the deepest faith, the most tender care, or the most vehement wishes can guarantee success. Imbolc symbolizes beginnings; if the opening goes badly wrong, the whole can be soured.

I have learned that life is easier when I don't expect too much. Imbolc—like its opposite Festival Lammas where the harvest is ready but yet to be secured—is all about expecting and even needing the best result. What happens may be largely up to chance. So when I write my blessings on ribbons

I try to confine their sentiments to what's possible or likely, as well as what's desirable. Maybe this is the challenge of Imbolc, to trust what happens next will be good. The Winter Solstice is a miracle, the departing sun returns. Imbolc, one station further around the Wheel, asks us to throw our weight behind this increasing light—planting seeds if we're living an agrarian life; committing to a course of action; and expending our energy, will power, hard work, and hope without guarantee.

Perhaps Imbolc is not simple at all, but the most important learning: after darkness comes light inevitably, unstoppably, and even ruthlessly. It's the insistence that we continue, even unknowing of the future. Newly hatched baby turtles make their death-defying dash for the sea, seedlings push up through the earth into daylight, and a new moon is born from the old. Celebrating this Festival wholeheartedly requires trust. Where is this trust to come from? We have to learn to trust in the Wheel itself; that it has turned, and will continue to turn. Imbolc has arrived, out of the darkness of the Winter Solstice. Imbolc's hope for the future is essential—it is the very turning of the Wheel and the life force itself.

Imbolc Memoir

It's been a long winter for me. It was not a winter of ice and snow, or even of long dark mornings and early evenings. I've been in a winter of relationships. I did have a summer, first; I was with a man I loved so deeply and with such joy I was catapulted out of everything I thought I knew about relationships. He taught me a way of being with another I had never known to even look for, where differences add together creating something neither could experience apart. One of his legacies for me is I am much happier in my relationship with my child. Another legacy has been that no matter whom I looked at afterward, that person and their promise did not begin to meet what I knew was possible.

People more sensible or pessimistic would probably just wait a year, two, or ten, or however long it took for that miracle to occur again. But I keep trying and trying to find a relationship—not the same one, which ended so badly—but one that blossoms and grows and has as its components love and trust and experiment and boldness bedded in a sense of the sacred. But it hasn't happened. I haven't found it. I carry this with me every day and in every ritual, but at Imbolc it seems particularly sharp. The Wheel has turned into the new; why can't I turn with it?

Our ritual is hinged around a song our ritual group wrote together; we pitched it together from remnants, scraps of other songs and ideas. What's this season about? It's about the new, taking a breath of fresh air, embodiment, and emerging from the dream-dark winter. It's about watching the world come to life again and allowing ourselves to arrive into a new stretch of our lives. I want the song to be made of discrete pieces. A chant that starts singing itself, with each fragment of each line creating a meaning that expands and expands the longer it's sung.

> *Breathing in, singing out*
> *Birth of new we bring about*
> *Singing out, breathing in*
> *Live the dream, let change begin.*

With a drumbeat we begin to find a rhythm for the song. *It has to be like breath,* I say, *breathy. As if you could breathe it, as well as singing it.*

We cast the circle into eight points, calling on the qualities of the land in each direction. The small beach with the winds and waves, the rocky cliff with dolphins playing below, the river mouth meeting the sea, the high lookout point where the whole area's laid out to be seen, ancient mountain, the beautiful lake, the sacred ceremonial ground, and the cave with the waterfall.

Breathing in, singing out. We start by breathing together. Imbolc is the time to take a deep breath, the breath after the birth of the Winter Solstice, maybe the first breath. The light was born again at midwinter, now it's time for us to emerge. It's time to greet fresh air. Our breath is the very first of the early spring breezes, stirring things up. We're receiving new springtime smells, brought on the wind. And what else would we do with this breath except sing? We breathe in and we sing out.

I breathe with the earth; I share this absolutely elaborate, incredibly simple breath with the plants, with other animals, with the living earth herself. I breathe in precisely what the plants have breathed out. I breathe out—or sing out—exactly what the plants need to breathe in. Together we are the earth's lungs, her breath. Our breath serves functions way beyond our own breathing or the lives of humans. These breaths sustain the plants, whose breathing has sustained ours; and the whole process begins to look like the planet is breathing, through us.

Birth of new we bring about. Singing, we form a line, youngest to oldest and join hands. Chanting the song in unison we begin the process. Trinda as the eldest is our anchor, standing with her legs wide apart while Damon as the youngest crawls through, emerging as if from a cave, from hibernation, from the deep earth. We do it slowly, ritually, striving to keep hold of each other's hands though the process isn't elegant or smooth. Apart from Damon, no one has a spare hand to help them crawl through and the people on either side have to remain crouched on the ground, shuffling forward or back to accommodate this process. Quite a few are larger than Trinda, requiring a gymnastic calisthenics as they slide themselves through, while still holding hands with someone already through the gateway and someone yet to go through.

We pant our way through the song, struggling to get the words right, remember them, stay in tune, keep the timing. Every winter ends in this, this struggling through. Not just winters of cold and ice or of gloom and dark, with the waiting and waiting for light to come earlier in the morning to last longer into the afternoon; just like the many times and places throughout human history where each day would be measured against the remaining food supply, our personal winters, too, can be bleak, desperate, and seem to drag on forever. Winters of illness, crisis, or ended relationships; winters of the mind where depression sinks its teeth in and seems not to let go for a very long time; dull winters where our purpose gets forgotten in the drudgery and mundane; fierce winters where we can't imagine how to ever get through the loss of something that was maybe dearer to us than our own lives; terrifying winters facing mortality; and devastating winters of violent uprisings, wars, rebellions, or disasters (natural or otherwise).

Considering that a winter is worth recovering from, how do we pick our-selves up after those painful winters? Especially when we live with the risk it may happen again, and the knowledge that our lives might never be the same? How do I, having been broken-hearted, decide to open my heart again? How do parents give themselves to another child, having lost one? How do subsis-tence farmers plant the land again, when everything has been destroyed? How do refugees settle in a new land after leaving their homes and cultures behind? How do victims of rape, war, trauma, and abuse manage to put those experi-ences largely behind them? How do we allow ourselves to recover from illness, disability, disease, or crisis and emerge into a life beyond that place?

We are tugged there by the life in front of us by our children or our hope for the future. Sometimes we drag others along with us, people dependent on us or inspired by us. We let our bodies show the way, showing us how to recover from illness and compelling us to keep eating and breathing even though a loved one has died and will never breathe or eat again. The necessity of food for ourselves and our children forces us to plant again—or to flee or migrate to a place we can find nourishment. The desperate wishes for peace, freedom, equality, or a life for our children inspire us to continue even after the streets have been places of slaughter, homes have been broken in to and destroyed, or our fellow citizens have been beaten or tortured or murdered.

In the Imbolc ritual, I am in the middle of the line. When it is my turn, I crouch and crawl through incrementally in a shuffle crouched over, almost limply and partly sideways. The other hands clutched in mine both help and hinder. The song starts to break up in my mind, and all around me people are finding phrases they like, that are meaningful to them, and starting to chant them, recreating the chant between us but not one of us any longer singing the whole thing through. I hunch and shuffle and sing; the practical details of emerging make it harder than I imagined.

I had thought it would be impossible to reconstruct my life without the relationship. And I was so unfinished with it, so filled with hopes and plans and love and commitment, all going forward on a path that suddenly ceased to exist. I felt I was left with no path; I was endlessly mourning, filled with pain and regret. I had to force myself through the days. I promised that every day I would place a flower on my altar, which meant I had to go down from my third-floor flat and into the garden. I went to the beach and watched the moon rising, forty minutes or so later each day, getting up at two and three and four in the morning until I finally saw the most rarely seen moon, that slim crescent on the way to dark moon, visible for only ten or fifteen minutes before the sun rises. It was an emergence of something usually hidden, and watching it I discovered a new part of myself.

Singing out, breathing in. This is the bit of the chant catching at me, bringing me down and through, showing me the way. Still crouched on the floor, my head down I chant over and over again *Singing out, singing out, singing out.* I am offering myself to life, again and again. I am creating ritual, regardless of the weather or if I don't feel like it or am not inspired, regardless if anyone comes, whether the ritual takes hold with magic fierceness in a moment and burns or whether it does not. I am singing out.

I am trying to find a relationship that has meaning for me—depth, vibrancy, spirit, and a lasting support. I am singing out my needs, wishes, and songs to the universe and the Goddess. I am singing out my visions and ideas and words in writing, offerings, workshops, groups, and magical workings; *singing out.* And breathing in, so as to be able to sing the next bit. *Breathing in;* I forget that sometimes, to take comfort from the rocky cliffs, the cold river and clear night sky, in the moon rising and my child growing and my body that can still dance and laugh and work. To run the energy as a cycle, so I receive in equal measures to giving, that I am renewed in the singing out.

Live the dream, let change begin. I am out the other side, emerged now and coaching the next person through, finally half-standing again as the end of the line tries to twist itself inside out. I am still *singing out* and *singing out* among the other lines and phrases, all singing and blending and breathing together, but I also sing *let change begin* and I thread a new line together with *singing out, let change begin* weaving its way into the song we are making. I feel held at all points in this line—neither oldest nor youngest, just one in a line of emergence and singing—and the last people are struggling through, requiring that Trinda almost turn herself inside out. She bends over and twists around, finally spinning right around on one leg; her own whirling birth in the vortex.

Still holding hands we circle again, Trinda and Damon closing the last link. This is the dream. These rituals—living this cycle and holding Damon within it, turning the seasons together—this is my dream, alive. And it changes and changes and changes. Each time we do any ritual it's different. The weather and what's happening in the world and our lives; choosing pieces of rituals to keep, or enhance, or discard; exploring new ideas and incorporating further depths. Each time, I see different things and watch Damon grown another year to travel more strongly and deliberately in this pattern, rising and falling and coming forth one piece each time and revealing himself to himself.

When we finally stop singing we take the Lammas Dolly we made six months ago out to the orchard and place it in a tree as a sign of our faith in the coming season. We come back to the house and each receives a native seedling to put in the earth and assist this season of growth. I am born again within this simple Imbolc ritual; I am in love with each person now standing in the circle, all still singing together, reemerged into the possibility of love. *Singing out, singing out.* I am opening.

Hopes and Wishes

It is easy to associate with Imbolc when we look at three-, four-, five-, or six-year-olds. The intent way children look at life, fascination with a caterpillar's progress, a machine digging up the street, or the sweep of a lighthouse highlights their innocence. And yet if we give it a moment's consideration we would have to agree those things *are* fascinating; all those little legs of the caterpillar and its humping motion, not to mention the neat bites they take out of leaves and their stripes of amazingly intense color. And what exactly is under the street, anyway? And how does a digger work? A lighthouse is indeed mesmerizing. In fact, all these things are much more interesting than what to cook for dinner, the stress of office politics, or any past event we might be mulling over, or future event we might be worrying about. A child's interests are about what's happening in the present.

Small children—whose feet rush them over to what's most intriguing, whose eyes widen as if to take in more and more of life, whose hands reach out to grab and touch and discover, whose endless questions seek not to confirm what they know—are guides to the themes of Imbolc. When we are at the beginning of things—such as the start of a love affair; stepping for the first time into a foreign country; discovering meditation, music, or art—we are in Imbolc mind.

The hope and wonder that exist during those moments are not tempered by our knowledge of harsh realities, which take a back seat while we revel in the freedom of discovery. And even if we have done something before, it does not detract from the experience of beginning the experience again. We are so fully committed to the experience we don't consider either the past (what may have happened to us in similar or related situations) or the future (what may well happen, according to our knowledge of the world and ourselves).

This childlike state of being is exactly what Imbolc calls for. For each child, discovering the world is new. Each spring is the first spring; there has never been *this* spring. This spring, that combines both the archetype of all springs plus the particulars of this, unique and once-only spring. Each love affair is the first love affair. Although thousands of people have written about what it is like to fall in love, and most of us have read in books and poems and heard songs about other people's versions of falling in love, it's only as we experience it that we understand it.

It's a state of mind to which children have constant access and the rest of us experience in short bursts during emotionally intense situations that are new to us. The beginner's mind is Imbolc mind, a state of being where the possible difficulties of the future are not admitted. It also has very little reference to the past. If we remembered the results of the last time we fell in love or anticipated some of the likely future outcomes, we would no longer be experiencing that rush of being in love. Imbolc is often illustrated with a picture of a snowdrop; a single brave flower with its bright green stem and single white bell surrounded by snow. If that snowdrop knew another heavy snowfall might occur, or the snow was likely to turn to ice, it wouldn't be so keen—but it doesn't know. Another image associated with this season is newborn lambs. If they understood half of them would be in the abattoir in a few months they wouldn't frolic so happily, or look so idyllic, but they also don't know.

These moments of not knowing can result in some extraordinary insights and inspirations. Falling in love we might feel at one with everyone who's ever fallen in love. Arriving in a new country we might understand how the life we have created for ourselves is just a convenient set of structures that doesn't represent our true desires. At the beginning of new spiritual practices we often have powerful experiences and receive stunning insights. And each Imbolc we can be struck anew with how extraordinary the world is, how fragile and beautiful our ecosystem is, and how amazing each breath is.

Small children have an original view of the world; not so much that the things they say have never been thought or said before, but they express them uniquely. At age four, Damon asked me how many arms the Goddess had. When I asked for his opinion he addressed himself seriously to the question. *She doesn't have any arms*, he said, *because she is the earth. And she has lots of arms, because she is Kali.* I could hardly have come up with any better answer, no matter my years of learning, reading, and work I had done. He spoke with beginner's mind.

I took Damon to Europe when he was four. While in Paestrum, Italy, we visited the Temple of Ceres. I would say, *This is a temple of Ceres*, and then I would try to erase from my mind the history of what had happened to that temple, the Goddess religion of the people who built it, and how the temple had become ruins; it had been largely neglected even as a tourist attraction. But Damon would lift his head up and for him it *was* Ceres's temple. It was not ruins. It had no other history. It was alive, living in him, and I was envious seeing in him the immediacy and reverence for an actual temple of the Goddess, right this minute, as we stood in it.

When Damon was six, we went to Turkey. In Ephesus, speeding ahead of the adults into the museum, he let out a kind of choked cry. *She's here!* he said, and his voice was awe and splendor and huge satisfaction and he raced through the first room and around the corner into a parallel room where three multi-breasted Artemis statues stood. He had glimpsed her through an internal arch-like window between the two rooms and seen—not what adults would see, the stupendously beautiful statue of Artemis as the mother of all life, crawling with bees and animals and breasts enough to feed the world—but the Goddess herself. To Damon, she was there, physically and energetically present.

I've heard plenty of Pagans and read of many others who keep their children separate from their religion. They say the children will have a chance to choose when they get older. How odd it is I've never heard a devout Catholic or Jew proclaiming this, or read of Muslims raising their children free of religion, to be able to choose when they get older. Except for in an oppressive political or social regime, raising someone within a belief system doesn't appear to take away anyone's ability to choose beliefs for themselves as they get older. In some rare instances, Pagan parents have feared losing their children to the other parent or even the state due to their beliefs and practices. This is not the norm. But while other Pagans continue to conceal what they do even from their own children, it's hard to argue the Pagan spirituality is just another expression of diverse spirituality.

I advocate to include our children in our reverence and celebrations, allowing them to observe alongside us as we practice what is dearest to us. They should be able to question, criticize, mimic, participate in, or otherwise respond to these practices as they see fit. The very basic tenet of Paganism is that it relies on direct experience rather than abstract faith or written lore. This tenet surely protects one who chooses to have their spiritual experiences elsewhere, or to not have them at all. The concept of choice is easily included within Pagan practice. Unless you live in a very unusual situation, children will be constantly bombarded with other religious beliefs; it will hardly be any surprise to them that there are other ways of thinking. Paganism has much to give, whether or not the child chooses it later in life.

Children love rituals—from decorating a Christmas tree to icing a birthday cake to making a Lammas Dolly. The very things that adults often struggle with during a ritual—disbelief, self-criticism, fear of looking foolish, a loathing or dread of singing and dancing—don't even occur to children. Children are wonderful role models. They are also perfectly happy with ideas of talking to trees, getting messages from birds that happen to fly overhead, and understanding natural patterns and rhythms. This kind of innocence is intrinsic to nature religions.

When I tell children the four elements are everywhere, all the time, they immediately set about finding them much more confidently than many adults, wherever they happen to be. Adults easily come to think of the elements as a candle and a chalice on the altar, but children look around and point to the sun for fire; they reason that plants are storing water, or point to clouds on the horizon. This is an Imbolc mind—a fresh, open mind, a growing mind. There has been the Winter Solstice—birth—and now Imbolc—growth. A child, just like a seedling, will absorb whatever it can from its surroundings to nourish it.

Paganism is a fairly simple religion, although practicing it in most of today's societies is not necessarily simple. Still, it's not hard to explain to a child. There are no great leaps of faith or logic involved, no punishments threatening those who stray, and no obscure books of lore that contradict themselves. The teacher is nature itself, and children identify with and enjoy nature more simply and immediately than many of their parents. Paganism could be called an Imbolc religion, in that it has a kind of wondrous, fresh naivety about it. Theory and practice are not separate. There is no higher authority to call upon, unless one calls on the Gods or the earth. Like nature in early spring, like Imbolc, Paganism is creative, often spontaneous, diverse, self-managing, chaotic, and optimistic. It calls for trust in both the natural world and the cycles of life.

Imbolc Ritual

Notes: "Ritual Basics" on page 295 covers many aspects of ritual, including grounding, casting circles, invocations, and participation.

Making blessing ribbons is described in more detail on page 79.

Section 6, "Looking to the Future," is the central part of this ritual.

Ask everyone to bring:

- Two ribbons, each 20 inches (50 centimeters) long and at least a half-inch or one centimeter wide. White or brightly colored, not dark

- Two natural items that can easily be tied onto a ribbon (for example, a shell with a hole in it, a feather, a seedpod, or a sturdy flower)

- Food for the Imbolc Feast if you are having one

Other things needed for this ritual:

- Good marking pens (narrow felt-tip pens are best)

- Some backup ribbons and extra natural items to tie on them

- A candle, which can be on a simple altar

- A bowl or other container for the natural items .

- If there are no trees or bushes outside where the blessing ribbons can be tied, a branch or other arrangement will be needed inside

- Last season's Lammas Dolly, if you have one

- A gift of seeds for the group; alternatively use seedlings of native plants, vegetables, or flowers

- Drum/percussion instrument (one or more)

Clothing suggestion:

- White or cream

Roles in ritual:

These can be done by different people or one or two people can take all or most of the roles depending on how confident and experienced the group is:

- Casting the circle and calling directions, which can be done by several different people or all by one person

- Grounding

- Leading warm-ups

- Leading discussion and giving instructions

- Timekeeper (this may not be necessary, or can be combined with another role)

- Drummer/song leader

- Facilitators for each of the age related groups (optional—good for a very large group). Divide these groups as appropriate for the people expected. One option is ages 0–20; 21–40; 41+. To get roughly equal numbers in each group, we sometimes divide ages 0–16; 17–45; 46+

Length of Ritual: 1.5 hours

Ritual

1. Gathering

Welcome the group to the ritual space and take care of any housekeeping. If some people are unfamiliar with ritual etiquette, briefly explain how you'd like the ritual to run.

Announce the intention of the ritual. This could be, *This ritual is to celebrate Imbolc, the beginning of spring, Our intention today is to invoke blessings for the year that's unfolding,* or *Welcome to this Festival of youth and growth.*

Ask everyone to introduce themselves briefly. Start with yourself, to give a demonstration of the type of introduction you want. If you have a large group (over twenty), you can ask people simply to introduce themselves to the person or people next to them.

2. Grounding and Warm-ups

Warm-ups are optional, but great in a group that doesn't know each other well, isn't practiced in ritual, or in groups with children.

GROUNDING:

- Briefly introduce the idea of grounding and explain that it is done to assist everyone to become more present, feel alive in their bodies, and release distractions.

- Offer a seasonal grounding based on a bird hatching out of an egg, or sap spreading through a tree to provoke new growth and leaves unfurling. Ask each person to feel their own sap rising, or their wings stretching out to dry.

- Speak slowly and clearly, adding intonation and variety to your voice as your grounding evolves.

- Finish with a clear instruction for everyone to open their eyes (if participants' eyes were shut) and become fully present.

SUGGESTED WARM-UPS:

- **Physical:** Beginning life; become birds in shells, breaking your way out. Then become new seeds cracking open and seeking light and air. Then become flowers ripening into bud and bloom.

- **Vocal:** Navigate by sound; with eyes closed, each person emits a low, constant sound while moving about the space slowly, trying to avoid bumping into others by using hearing alone.

3. Creating a Sacred Space

- **Cast a circle:** If you want to give your circle casting a magical Imbolc flavor, have each child walk around the space carrying an element. For example, one child carries a candle, another a chalice of water. Otherwise have someone walk around the perimeter of the circle using a hand or magical tool to draw the outline of the circle.

- **Call to the directions and the elements:** For this ritual, assign four people and have them each call to a Cross-Quarter and then have them call Above and Below all together. You can also work with eight people, one in each of the quarters and cross quarters. You may wish to have people of distinctly different ages calling the directions; children for the northeast in the Northern Hemisphere (southeast in the Southern Hemisphere), someone in their twenties or thirties for the southeast in the Northern Hemisphere (northeast in the Southern Hemisphere), someone around their forties for the southwest in the Northern Hemisphere (northwest in the Southern Hemisphere), and an older person for the northwest in the Northern Hemisphere (southwest in the Southern Hemisphere). This can also be done by a single person (and in that case, stay with the four Cross-Quarters as Imbolc is a Cross-Quarter Festival).

Northern Hemisphere:

Northeast	Imbolc, stirrings of new life, breeze and the soil awakening
East	Winds bringing fresh air and change
Southeast	Sap rising, stirred by the sun
South	Warming sun, promise of light lengthening
Southwest	Seeds forming that will become grain and crops
West	Rains, feeding life
Northwest	Pattern of life and growth, encoded in each living creature
North	Renewal of the earth, as life awakens

Above and Below

Southern Hemisphere:

Southeast	Imbolc, stirrings of new life, breeze and the soil awakening
East	Winds bringing fresh air and change
Northeast	Sap rising, stirred by the sun
North	Warming sun, promise of light lengthening
Northwest	Seeds forming that will become grain and crops
West	Rains, feeding life
Southwest	Pattern of life and growth, encoded in each living creature
South	Renewal of the earth, as life awakens

Above and Below

4. Introducing Imbolc

Have one person stand forward and speak about Imbolc. Explain where it fits into the Wheel of the Year and that the Cross-Quarters are often considered more important, seasonally, than the equinoxes and solstices.

Imbolc is the Festival opposite to and balancing Lammas. The agricultural themes of growth and death—especially in the life cycle of seeds—are picked up and begun here and completed in Lammas. It is also very much a season of youth; the birth of animals, hatching of birds, sprouting of new plant life and renewal of plants that have been dormant through winter. You might like to include local information, relevant to what is happening where you are.

After the initial explanation, ask each person to contribute their own ideas about what Imbolc or this time of the year means to them. It may mean the mornings are getting lighter, or the beginning or ending of a school term, or that it's time to get back into the vegetable garden. If it is a large group (over twenty people), you can break into smaller groups for this.

You may wish to include in the discussion the aspect of Imbolc as a time of youth, promise, and blessings with relevance to real-life situations, such as beginning new projects, looking after a young family, or turning a corner in a difficult issue. Bringing the themes of the Wheel of the Year closer to home can be done in a second round of sharing and will make the ritual more relevant and immediate.

5. Learning the Chant

Introduce the chant or chants you will be using later in the ritual. There are many chants on CDs, online, and in songbooks. You may already have favorite chants that are well-known to your group. You might also have a songwriter among you. Choose a simple song or chant that is true to the themes of your ritual and teach it to the group by singing it a couple of times and then teaching it line by line. It's useful to sing it through together at least eight or ten times, so when you begin singing later in the ritual everyone can easily join in without being having to be reminded of the words or tune.

6. *Looking to the Future*

Depending on what ages people are, divide the group into three age-related groups. Make sure the youngest group includes one or two teens or young adults who are confident facilitating (otherwise an adult can come into this group to assist). The groups have about twenty to thirty minutes together, and their presentations should last between two to five minutes.

The youngest group then has time to talk about their visions of the future and devise a presentation that will show their wishes. They can make up a short play, use movement, song, or any combination of activities.

The middle-aged group are asked to discuss their past actions in reference to creating a positive, sustainable, peaceful, and earth-friendly future, and then to discuss their forward paths, what each of them still hopes and plans to contribute in the future. This can first be done in pairs and later within the whole group. They then create a presentation to express this; it can take the form of a song, a small play, a dance, or any other offering.

The oldest group forms a council to discuss what they can offer and how they plan to support the youngest group (as a group rather than as individuals). They then create a presentation to express this, using storytelling, mime, movement, or anything else.

Each group enacts their presentation for the others, with the youngest going first.

7. *Blessing Ribbons*

This activity is fully described on page 79, immediately after the ritual.

Gather in a group and give clear instructions for the next part of the ritual.

Light the candle, if it wasn't already lit. Every person then puts their two natural items into a bowl on or near the altar. Ask each person (children may need help) to write a blessing on each of their two ribbons; both must be blessings they would be delighted to receive. For example, *The blessing of a bountiful year, The blessing of good health,* or *The blessing of true love.* After this is done, everyone stands in a circle with their two ribbons held in one hand at head height. This process provides a great time to chant, particularly if you have a large group.

The first person crosses the circle and takes one ribbon from someone else (without knowing what it says) and adds it to their own two ribbons. They then sit down or stand back from the circle; the person who now has only one ribbon crosses the circle to take one ribbon from someone else. The two ribbons they are now holding are their final ribbons, so they also sit or stand back from the group. The crossing and choosing continues with the next person, who was left with only one ribbon. This repeats until everyone has exchanged a ribbon. For the final pair, the person who began rejoins the circle with their three ribbons, one of which is then chosen by the person who was left with only one.

Everyone now has their blessings for the year. Once each has read their blessings, they step forward, a few at a time, and choose one of the natural objects for each ribbon to anchor the blessing. This may be a purely aesthetic choice or have some meaning. For example, a blessing of *Freedom* may have a feather tied to it to indicate flight or the freedom of the air.

Each person then chooses one of their blessings to offer to the world, and one to take for themselves into the coming year. The blessings for the world should be offered in whichever way you have chosen.

8. Raising Energy

If you have a drummer or percussionist, they can lead into the song. Start gently, reminding others of the words and tune and gradually increase the energy of the song. Turn it into a round if you like.

This is the time to raise energy if you plan to. You may also choose to do a spiral dance or another dance of your preference.

9. Complete the Ritual

Thank and acknowledge the directions in the reverse order that they were called and dissolve the circle. Generally the same people who cast and called do this.

- Acknowledge the directions:

Northern Hemisphere:

Below and Above

North	Renewal of the earth, as life awakens
Northwest	Pattern of life and growth, encoded in each living creature
West	Rains, feeding the growth of life
Southwest	Seeds that are sprouting, that will become grain and crops
South	Warming of the sun, promise of light lengthening
Southeast	Sap rising, stirred by the sun
East	Winds bringing in fresh air and change
Northeast	Imbolc, the stirrings of new life, breeze and the soil awakening

Southern Hemisphere:

Below and Above

South	Renewal of the earth, as life awakens
Southwest	Pattern of life and growth, encoded in each living creature
West	Rains, feeding the growth of life
Northwest	Seeds that are sprouting, that will become grain and crops
North	Warming of the sun, promise of light lengthening
Northeast	Sap rising, stirred by the sun
East	Winds bringing in fresh air and change
Southeast	Imbolc, the stirrings of new life, breeze and the soil awakening

- **Dissolve the circle:** If a circle was cast, the same person or people walk around it in the opposite direction, gathering up the energy, or otherwise dispersing it. If your circle was cast by children, they may skip or run back around the circle.

Thank each person for coming and for what they have contributed. If you have a gift of seeds or seedlings, give them out now and begin your Imbolc Feast if you are having one.

Imbolc Activity: Blessing Ribbons

You can make Imbolc Blessing Ribbons as part of larger ritual or as a stand-alone ritual by yourself or with others. This is a simple charm in keeping with the energy of the season. It can be done quickly and easily, or given more depth if you want to make a ceremony of it. You can use the opportunity to reflect on blessings you already have or might like to give others.

Feel free to vary the ritual as you like. You could tie ribbons onto trees without anything written on them or attach feathers to the ribbons and leave them catching the breeze as a blessing for the land and the trees. For small children, the color of the ribbons will be a more powerful symbol than words. Let them suggest the meanings of the colors; they might decide blue is for love and green is for happiness. You may wish to make the link not just with blessings for the earth but also with water by tying ribbons into a tree or bush near a spring, pond, or stream. This time of year is often associated with sacred wells.

Use cotton or satin ribbons and be aware of any environmental impact you might be creating. You might want to come back in a few months and let the blessings go by untying the ribbons, taking them home, and disposing of them. In other places (such as your own backyard) it may be fine to leave them there, even adding next year's ribbons to the same tree. In a large garden, you may have each person tie their ribbon to whichever tree they are drawn to, and have blessings fluttering across a wide area. If you wish to avoid involving trees at all, the ribbons can all be tied to a string like prayer flags, either outdoors or inside near a window.

You will need:
- 2 ribbons for each person, each 20 inches or 50 centimeters long and at least half an inch or one centimeter wide; white or another color, but not black. If you are doing this as a solo ritual, you might choose to work with more than two blessings and will need the appropriate number of ribbons

- Natural items that can easily be tied onto a ribbon; for example, a shell with a hole in it, a feather, seedpod, or a special leaf. You will need at least one for each ribbon, and it's good to have a few extras

- One or more narrow felt-tip marking pen, as needed

- A candle to light during the making of the blessings (if you choose)

- Somewhere to put the finished blessings (see above)

Time:
- 30 minutes

Intention

Decide what the purpose and intent of the blessings are to be. If you are working alone, with just a few adults, or with older children, you can leave this decision until you start. If you're working with a big group or with small children, it's better if you know what the intention of the blessings is to be (blessings for the earth, blessings for oneself, or blessings for others) and also where they will go once they are made, whether that is outside, inside, home with the person, exchanged with other people, or any combination of these. When people are making two blessings each, it's easy to double up on this (take one home and hang one in a tree or give one to another person and keep the other).

Method

- You may like to speak a little about the time of year, and the themes of Imbolc.

- If you want to explore the nature of blessings, you can ask each person what blessings they have in their life or what blessings they seek to give others. Most children are happy to explore such a concept once you've given a few clear examples. Children may count as blessings something we would not call a blessing.

- Explain how the blessings will be made and what will be done with them.

- Speak briefly about selecting colors of ribbons for blessings and the decoration; for example, a blessing of clean waters might be written on a blue ribbon with a shell attached, or a blessing of growth and learning may be written on a green ribbon with a seedpod attached. If you have children present, encourage them to think of some examples.

- Each person chooses their ribbons and writes their blessings on them, usually a different blessing on each. Then they choose a natural object to go with each blessing and tie it on the end of the ribbon. Children may need an adult to do the writing. You may also choose to forgo writing on the ribbon and let the color and object speak for themselves. All blessings should be expressed in the most positive way; for example, *I bless you with good health* rather than *May you recover from your illness.*

- Do whatever it is you've decided to do with the blessings; tie them all to a branch or exchange them with each other (so that the blessings you receive are a surprise).

- It's lovely to have each person read out the blessings they've received, or talk about the process of sharing blessings.

Spring Equinox

Celebrated on or close to March 21 in the Northern Hemisphere
and September 21 in the Southern Hemisphere.

Spring Equinox

The Spring Equinox has often marked my return to Australia. Many times it's been a definite date to set against my wandering and I've arrived home just in time for this ritual. It reminds me of Persephone who also arrives in spring when she emerges from the Underworld. Though I was returning from the Northern Hemisphere's summer, I was also emerging from a secret, traveling life, returning to my more mundane Australian life. Like Persephone, most of the secrets I carried with me weren't translatable. I had to become two different people, with parallel lives that I dipped in and out of as I traversed the hemispheres.

Spring Equinox is my Festival of return and that's what I celebrate with Persephone. The return always has mixed blessings. It's a time of confrontation. What's happened to my relationships while I've been away? Have the people staying in my house looked after it? What work can I create? Sometimes the answers have been that the relationships no longer exist, the house is filthy and the garden neglected, and there's hardly any work for me in Australia. I would come home fueled up, filled with visions, experiences, and my most exciting events and no one in my ordinary life could really relate to it much. That was elsewhere. In spite of arriving at the Spring Equinox, it felt like I went into retreat, parts of my life only emerging again when I departed.

The themes and emblems of Easter overlay those of the Spring Equinox. In the Northern Hemisphere it's easy to conflate the two. In Australia, Easter appears incongruously at the time of the Autumn Equinox. All the Pagan themes of Easter (bunnies, eggs, spring flowers, and rebirth) are hard to correlate with autumn, and make the inflexibility of the Christian church's calendric religion appear starkly irrelevant. Of course eggs and chocolate are lovely things, so we in the Southern Hemisphere compromise and have them twice a year with the autumn leaves on the harvest altar and again at the Spring Equinox in September.

Just once Damon and I had a Spring Equinox in England. I remember how concrete gray London had been, and how green buds and pink and white blossom—overnight it seemed—suddenly took the eye, startling against the drab buildings. Over Easter, we camped in some woods outside London. Damon was six and beside himself with excitement. There were actual rabbits! A woman living nearby appeared with a little basket filled with chocolate eggs for him, *and* it snowed! Damon was entranced and ever afterward, and even in Australia with no snow and no bunnies and no chocolate eggs (unless we had remembered to save some from Easter six months earlier), he retained his loyalty to the Spring Equinox as one of his favorite Festivals.

Every Spring Equinox, we paint boiled eggs elaborately with gold and silver paint, miniature poems, or entire cosmologies. Often we have an egg-painting party a day or two before the ritual with five or six people sitting around the table decorating a couple of eggs each, discussing technique and giving encouragement and advice. We've had phoenix eggs with flames licking up them, spiraling snake eggs, spring flower eggs, rainbow eggs, moon and sun eggs, and just about anything else you can imagine.

Before the ritual begins we ask a couple of children to hide the eggs outside. Some they put in careful nests of grass, others wedged in the fork of a tree or nestled into the top of a tree fern. They balance them on outside window ledges and hide them against a veranda post or in the ground cover. During the ritual we have an egg hunt, and we believe the egg you choose will have something to tell you. Perhaps it reminds you to reach high for what you want, to fill your life with flowers and sunshine, or to risk rebirth like the phoenix. These eggs can last for months on our altars, although sometimes we've buried them in the ground, like seeds. My favorite egg ever I painted was deep blue with hints of silver stars and in the tiniest yellow writing I could manage, the words *secrets lie inside of me.* I was reluctant to give it up. But Damon, who hid the eggs, claimed it for himself in the egg hunt, so it didn't go very far.

Spring Equinox Memoir

It's September 2001 and I am back in Australia with Damon. We've been here only a few days. It took us a week to get out of New York plus a day flying across America in short flights and another twenty hours in Los Angeles because we missed our flight due to endless delays, false starts, and roundabout flight routes. When we got to Australia, I discovered we had to wait a further six hours for a flight home. I lay down on the floor in the airport and went to sleep, Damon by my side. My body still trembled in aftershock from flights, lack of sleep, and anxiety. Still, being in Australia again was a physical relief. New York was a strange place to be the week following September 11, 2001, and I hadn't let myself feel very much while I was there.

The Spring Equinox is a good time to come back. I always say that, but this time I am in a blank space, not processing anything I saw or felt in the previous two weeks. That's until I arrive at the ritual at a friend's home in the hills. When I get out of the car, I look across the gorge to the cliffs rearing up in the middle distance. They are beautiful layers of rock with trees, narrow waterfalls, all wilderness. But what I remember is standing outside on the departure level of LaGuardia Airport sometime past 9:00 a.m. on September 11, 2001, looking across the middle distance to the city of New York. I watched smoke pouring out of two towers, one collapsed and one still standing. I told nine-year-old Damon not to look. He sat on my feet instead, facing away and reading the fourth *Harry Potter* book. I hadn't wanted him to bring it because it was so heavy.

I thought I could be watching the beginning of a war. All around me people were questioning each other, trying to get phone reception or radio reception, searching for a way to get back home. The airport building behind us closed. There were no buses and no taxis. Someone came along and shouted for us to leave the airport, but I couldn't see why we'd be any safer a few hundred yards up the street. A great inertia came over me. I hoped the United States government didn't know who'd done it so they wouldn't be able to retaliate instantly. I hadn't planned to be standing on the doorstep of the next war. I thought ironically of the times my father had ineffectually warned me against traveling to Egypt or Turkey. No one expected the land of the free to be so unsafe.

I wondered—as I watched the second tower, just in case I was about to die—what mattered most. I caught sight of a three-quarter waning moon partway up the sky. Just for a moment, I turned my head slightly to look at it. The dinosaurs saw that moon. And I knew that tomorrow, no matter what happened down here on the ground, the moon would rise and continue on its cycle whether we were here or not. It comforted me. I felt strengthened.

I turned back to the towers. I had been looking at the moon for maybe thirty seconds, but when I looked back the second tower wasn't there. Incredibly, given my vantage point and how little else I was doing, I missed it. We were just eight kilometers away. I had Damon with me; I knew I ought to be doing something responsible. I coaxed him into standing and wheeling his suitcase, and we slowly moved off the ramp and down to ground level where a small sea of people milled and asked questions. I had never been to this airport before and had no idea which direction to head in or what was nearby. We found a piece of grass and sat down, somewhere on the road heading out of the airport, and I shut down. It's not how I thought I'd be in an emergency, but my brain literally wasn't operating. I felt lost, adrift; my awareness reduced down to the very small circle of Damon and me. Waiting.

When I get out of the car at the Spring Equinox ritual and see those cliffs, the incongruence is too great. It's autumn back where I've just come from— the season of reckoning. Thousands of people died in the incident I was so close to; hundreds of them as the second tower collapsed while I stood watching the moon. Returning to spring is too much for me. I open the back of the car and get in and lie down. I start crying, really crying for the first time since it happened. All those people, dead, in the thirty seconds it took me to glance up at the moon.

While I was still in the United States, I stayed rational. They planned the timing of it—you can't deal with flights and not know the exact time things will happen—and they planned it to hit before 9 a.m., before most people were at work. It was a warning, a nasty and dramatic warning, but they chose a death toll thousands lower than it would have been just an hour later. Still, I tried to get us out of the United States as fast as I could. I didn't trust their response and I didn't want to be in the middle of it. I looked at Europe and Canada in case I couldn't get back to Australia in that long, uneasy week of hysteria that gradually resolved into a cautious, rewritten world. Day by day we seemed to creep away from the precipice threat of outright war into some ferocious but more oblique response.

We found refuge in some friends' flat in New York. While Damon and their son built a Lego-world in the bedroom they refused to leave, I stayed alert enough to monitor the options, searched for an opening, and seized it when it came—the first plane bound for Australia out of the States. We could get on it because, miraculously, that had been our departure date and we held valid tickets for that flight. All we had to do was get from New York to Los Angeles. Three small airlines patched flights together that we hadn't paid for to allow us to get there.

It was like a shock wave reached out from the towers, hitting me all the way from New York. Only now I am back in Australia staring at these cliffs, and I am helpless in it. I can't do anything. I certainly can't run a ritual. After a while, people start to come and see me, one at a time, where I lie in the back of the car. *I can't do it*, I say. *I was there. I saw it.* I am shaking, trembling, in shock, still crying. No one seems that interested. *You can wait a while*, they say. *Not everyone's here yet. Will you be okay in fifteen minutes?*

Half an hour later I am still not okay. All I can see is the shimmering space where that tower was, those people. I'm grateful it waited this long to really reach me, but I feel the threads of their lives, sudden ghosts wavering in the air, displaced. I was a witness; I have to hold space for them. I didn't pay them much attention at the time, those deaths, all I could think about—and not very well—was what to do for Damon and me.

Eventually, after many people had left the airport, a young man came along. He was how I'd always imagined I would be in an emergency. He'd gone looking for options and he'd discovered there was a hotel not far away. He'd come back for anyone who needed help, encouragement, directions, or support. He said he was going to the hotel, and he'd take anyone who wanted to come. A few people gathered about him, including an old couple whose luggage he managed, a slightly hysterical woman who leaned on his arm, and some uncertain hangers-on. He encouraged us to keep walking. *Not far now*, he said. He was noble, weighted down by us, and I was tremendously grateful to him for his resourcefulness and for bothering about anyone else. Damon and I silently trailed with him, part of his small group of dependents, to the hotel where there were hundreds of people camped in the hallways. We found a tiny space against a door and put our things down, marking out our little place. The hotel gave us sandwiches.

People at the ritual get more impatient. They come back to the car, where by now I am sitting up, looking at the cliffs. They're still waiting for me.

Why can't they run the bloody ritual themselves? I've never felt less like prancing around with eggs and whatever else we're supposed to be doing. I don't care who the Butterfly Goddess is, and the children can surely organize some games without me. Eventually someone I barely know comes out. He puts his hands on my shoulders and looks me in the eyes. He's gentle with me. He says Damon has hidden the eggs in the bamboo grove, and couldn't I just come and start them on the ritual?

I tell him what happened, what I saw. He nods. He can tell it's serious, but he doesn't seem to think it's a reason not to run the ritual. I decide to trust him, like that other young man who knew what to do in a crisis, and we go in and start the ritual. We cast a circle, we talk about the Spring Equinox. We choose a Butterfly Goddess and she's delighted to be chosen. The activities of the ritual unfold.

I've been away for months and only back a week or so, yet here are all these people—friends, my women's group, kids, people who sometimes come, and people who've never been before—gathered to celebrate one of these rituals I'm so dedicated to. They bring their painted eggs, their singing voices, and their willingness. It begins to seem quite amazing. I don't worry about Damon here, I can leave him alone for hours and the most that will happen is he'll get on with the ritual and hide the eggs in the bamboo grove. It's almost physically difficult, feeling safe; it's so jarring with what was and could have been. Instead there are cliffs with trees and birds, a bamboo grove with an egg hunt, and the Butterfly Goddess.

Over the Pacific Ocean, in the post-9/11 United States, I was lost and no one special, just another displaced traveler. After the hotel we had been taken on buses to a YMCA with hundreds of camp beds laid out in rows on a vast indoor field of basketball courts. I'd chosen a bed next to the wall and I lay on it, shrunken into myself while Damon read *Harry Potter* in the next bed. In the afternoon, a young man stopped by and asked if he could help. The place was filled with hundreds of distressed travelers, a whole group who only spoke Chinese, people who were terrified, people whose holidays were ruined, and people who were separated from their homes and families. They all wanted things. I asked him for a towel. After a while he came back with a thin white towel. It seemed like one of the nicest things anyone had done for me, ever.

The ritual starts to break through to me. I am directing it vaguely, but that's good enough; these people know how to be in ritual and as it's the Spring Equinox it's all dancing and celebration, nothing too difficult. But small things grab my eye. The look on a woman's face as she sings for the Goddess. A man crouched down to help the children compose their piece, listening earnestly as they all talk at once. A cross child, arguing with his mother and storming outside; these things nearly make me weep. I think again of Persephone, carrying both those different realities inside her, transiting between the two.

When we head outside for the egg hunt, I ask everyone to look forward, to imagine this egg represents the next six months as we swing into the light half of the year. I don't feel ready for that; I don't feel oriented at all with this side of the globe, heading into summer, far away from a possible war and the escalation of hostilities between the United States and the Middle East. But I'm here. And three months ago, on the Winter Solstice, I signed a contract for a house; it's half-finished on a large piece of land. I've got this child to look after and rituals to run, friends and a community I'm involved with. I head out to the bamboo grove to look for my egg; perhaps it will be painted with butterflies, or a waterfall, or a waning moon in a pale sky.

Balance and Light

When the Wheel of the Year is plotted over a compass, the Spring Equinox falls in the east in both hemispheres. It is the direction that will mean you witness the rising sun if you turn to face it at dawn. It varies from southeast to northeast at different times of the year, and it depends how far from the equator you are as to how great the variance, but the sun rises in the east every day. It is the tangible, visible reminder that after darkness comes light. The Spring Equinox aligns with the rising sun.

This Festival has an intrinsic sense of newness and freshness; everything that was just hinted at during Imbolc is now here in full swing. The Spring Equinox is representative of a very powerful thread in our religious and spiritual make-up; it is the emblem of the ever-returning, risen light. It's the new light of dawn, not a blazing overhead sun or one gently setting westward into the sea. It's more glaringly obvious than that subtle midnight moment of the Winter Solstice, when we have to believe the sun will return. Here it is written largely in flower buds, green leaves, birds hatching out of eggs, and the hours of daylight being equal again to those of night.

I've long thought the great fondness for the direction of east in Pagan and magical circles is because the whole of the Western Occult traditions—drawn from Egyptian, Greek, Jewish, and Roman writings, practices, and beliefs from which Christianity also arose—are aligned with this eastern view of the rising sun. Those religions style themselves as light-bringing where light represents knowledge, wisdom, and truth. These faiths also display strong preferences for mind and spirit over body, and even the idea that the mind and spirit are separate from the body.

We are a culture dedicated to light. Dark is cast as evil in popular parlance and even in psychological literature it is portrayed as a *shadow* (seen from the perspective of the light, presumably) that has to be integrated, not an honored realm with its own validity. Our whole way of thinking is opposed to the dark; as can be seen in our upward and onward focus, our view of life as a linear progression, and our denial of death. Yet the natural system teaches balance. There are as many days of winter as summer, as many hours of night as day within each year, and the moon is full only exactly as often as it is dark.

The concept of balancing light with dark seems difficult. Many of us expect that any darker parts of life will be kept to a minimum. They are viewed as automatically bad, and anyone who works willingly with the dark is suspect. Even when we say that dark is simply night—winter as opposed to summer; the time for rest, dreaming, and healing; and for the mysteries to reveal themselves—it's still rare to grant darkness half the field. And when we say that dark is also the place of initiation, of the Underworld and stripping away, letting go, to reemerge as changed, then it's even harder to give it equal time. If we say it is a place of the Dark Goddess, hidden truths, and our innermost selves, then often we don't want to offer it even a sliver of our attention.

Darkness is only *exactly* half of the equation at two points during the year, the Spring and Autumn Equinoxes. At all other points, darkness and light are imbalanced, with one greater than the other. Overall, they balance out. The days are longer in summer but shorter in winter; but these two equinoxes are the days of actual balance. Like any set of scales, the moment of equality is fleeting, but it is the moment deemed meaningful. Thus this balance at the Spring Equinox is celebrated as an important marker.

Working with my magical group, the Circle of Eight, we felt compelled to give darkness half our attention by virtue of the fact we followed the Wheel of the Year and that is what the seasons do. But it's noticeable that introducing the dark—even acknowledging it, sometimes—can be too much for some people. We believed shunning and ignoring the dark builds up shadow and projection. So, within careful parameters, we danced our rituals into the dark as fully as we did into the light. Occasionally, someone would say they found our Winter Solstice or Samhain rituals too dark, and parts of them did take place in actual darkness. Among other things, we visited the realms of the dead, named those who had died the previous year, invoked the Dark Goddess or Dark Lord, wore black and named our fears. Nothing was actually sinister, threatening, or overbearing, but if you're used to avoiding the dark, maybe even that is too much.

One year a couple in their early thirties came along to a couple of our circles. It happened to be around the time of the Spring Equinox and we were working with Persephone's story of emerging into spring. In the Spring Equinox ritual, we wove headdresses out of flowers and celebrated the light each one of us carries within. We invited Hades as well and discovered his compassion, giving up his beloved queen yearly to her springtime self. It was a moving ritual; sweet, light-filled, and strong. Afterward, the couple told us they'd decided not to continue in our circle, as we were too dark. We were amazed. What if they'd come to us at Lammas, or Samhain? What would they have thought then? And (searching our memories frantically), none of us could think of a single activity we'd undertaken with them that could be called dark. We hadn't invoked the Underworld, hadn't talked about death, hadn't explored our shadows or done any in-depth work at all.

We had to conclude, still mystified, that the mere notion of the dark *existing* or acknowledged in any way was too much for them. That all our circles and rituals contained some notion of balance, acceptance of the dark and they had picked this up, even at one of the brightest Festivals.

I don't feel it is possible to celebrate the seasons of the year or to do inner, personal, or magical work without recognizing darkness. We had no rebuttal for the couple—it was obviously better they never saw us in an actual dark part of the year. But we were left quizzically wondering if this intolerance for *any* darkness is endemic of our society. If that's true, it might be the greatest challenge as well as the greatest gift earth-centered spirituality offers to our current culture: the recognition of darkness as half of everything.

It seems so basic, this understanding; night is half and day is half. But of course, we get around that with electric light. Summer is half and winter is half; but we get around that with greenhouses, forcing fruit to grow before it is naturally growing in the season, cooling and heating rooms to our comfort with air conditioning and central heating. Winter hardly touches us. Night barely infringes upon our lengthy days. Death is compartmentalized and clinical, as is birth. Initiations are reduced to drunken parties and the intimacy of night is eaten up with television, working from home at all hours, and our nonstop communication devices. In that context, does a ritual like the Spring Equinox, which celebrates moving from the dark half of the year into the light, lose its significance?

In a human timeline, the Spring Equinox represents that extraordinary phase of beginning adult life, branching out from what we've been brought up with and finding our own way. It's stepping forward into our own life, as distinct from the way demonstrated by our parents. Those steps shine with potential and great visions; they seem bright and promising compared to what we've known, and perhaps what we've been led to expect. At this time of life we are making choices about relationships, work, and lifestyle; we are making our own mistakes and choosing how to deal with them and seeing the world as within our reach. It corresponds also to the time when hard work kicks in once a project is off the ground, or what happens when you turn up for a new job. It's filled with wonder and potential, but now we have to prove ourselves.

Perhaps it's not a phase we give much respect to—a part of life to be hurried through, not indulged. This phase is all so uncertain—which way will things go? We prefer to be further along the path, more established. The initial moment of something is fine—a business, a love affair, a baby—but then comes a difficult phase where the certainties are not established yet, a time that requires a lot of hard work if the goals are to come to fruition. This is hoeing the fields and planting the grain, for a potential harvest, much later. A possible harvest. If the weather's good, the Gods are kind, and plagues and wars don't come. A relationship, past that first flush of joy and union, has to enter a testing phase before it's really settled. Parents with a new baby receive an influx of attention, support, and delight. Then, long before the child can even walk or talk, all that's gone and they're left on their own on the enormously long road of parenting.

Remember what it was like to be twenty? Knowing mainly what you didn't want in life, not what you did? Feeling up against the mysterious forces that ruled the world, the ways of operation that everyone else knows about but you don't? Banking, contracts, politics, and philosophy. At the same time, you feel that all the choices in the world are yours, at least for a little longer. You're sure that your life won't contain the mistakes you see around you, that being grown up is both easier and more difficult than you'd ever thought. There's a pressure not to make mistakes, to be successful though you hardly know which direction you want to go in. Old friendships are falling away, outgrown; new ones are not quite there yet. Perhaps for the first time you're working with comparative vision, able to assess your aspirations, abilities, outlook on life, and upbringing.

Of all the Festivals, the Spring Equinox seems the brightest. The Spring Equinox is when the year takes that crucial step forward, out of darkness, and has a long stretch of increasing light ahead of it. It is not yet implicated in the Beltaine issues of fertility, which presage the death of its opposite point, Samhain; nor has it reached the full brightness of the Summer Solstice that lasts, really, only a moment before toppling over.

Yet this is not accorded its full significance. Ironically, our culture being dedicated to light has cast light-filled festivals into the shade; we don't find them very interesting. Because we've never acknowledged the dark properly, leaving it behind is not recognized. Thus, a Festival that is absolutely about the power of light gets lost in fluffy bunnies and colored eggs; nothing like the glory that should be accorded to it by right, if we were deeply in tune with the earth's cycles. The Spring Equinox has true wonder. It is a time of balance reached after darkness and uncertain beginnings, filled with the potential of the future.

Spring Equinox Ritual

Notes: "Ritual Basics" on page 295 covers many aspects of ritual, including grounding, casting circles, invocations and participation.

How to make Spring Equinox painted eggs is described on page 113. This ritual is written with alternative main sections. For a ritual with children, use section 6A, "Elemental Groups." Otherwise, use section 6B, "Future Visions." For each case, these sections will be the central part of the ritual.

Ask everyone to bring:

• A hard-boiled decorated or painted egg

• An offering for the Peace Altar

• Some inspiring words on peace

• Food for the Spring Equinox Feast, if you are having one

Other things needed for this ritual:

• Several extra decorated eggs

• Tiny chocolate eggs (optional)

• A Peace Altar in the center of the circle

• Music to dance to for option 6B

• Drum/percussion instrument (one or more)

Clothing suggestion:

• Each person to come dressed as an animal, bird, or plant

Roles in ritual:

These can be all done by different people or one or two people can take all or most of the roles depending on how confident and experienced the group is:

• Someone to hide the eggs, before the ritual begins. An older child will love to do this. Show the person clearly what area to hide the eggs and explain they should be at a variety of heights with some easy to find and retrieve and some not so easy. Ask them to remember where they put them in case their help is needed to find them again! Chocolate eggs, if you have them, can be hidden in the same area

• Casting the circle and calling directions (this can be done by several different people or all by one person)

• Grounding

• Leading warm-ups

• Leading discussion and giving instructions

• Timekeeper (this may not be necessary, or can be combined with another role)

• Drummer/song leader

- Facilitators for each of the elemental groups (optional, good for a very large group): air, fire, water, and earth (dressed appropriately)

Length of Ritual: 1.5 hours

Ritual

1. Gathering

Welcome the group to the ritual space and take care of any housekeeping. If some people are unfamiliar with ritual etiquette, briefly explain how you'd like the ritual to run.

Announce the intention of the ritual. For example: *Today we celebrate the Spring Equinox, The intention of this ritual is to cross from the dark half of the year to the light*, or *We come together for a Peace Ritual to help restore balance.*

Ask everyone to introduce themselves briefly. Start with yourself to give a demonstration of the type of introduction you want. If you have a large group (more than twenty), you can ask people simply to introduce themselves to the person or people next to them.

2. Grounding and Warm-ups

Warm-ups are optional, but are great in a group that doesn't know each other well or isn't practiced in ritual, and also in groups with children.

GROUNDING:

- Briefly introduce the idea of grounding, explaining that it is done to assist everyone to become more present, feel alive in their bodies, and release any distractions.

- Offer a seasonal grounding based on the balance between light and dark. Begin with feeling into the darkness of the earth below, the stillness, rest, and deep unfolding. Ask each person to imagine they have roots anchored there. Then introduce the idea of light, sunlight, and a balance to the dark. Suggest each person imagines they have branches stretching into the sky. Finally ask everyone to find a balance of light and dark within themselves.

• Speak slowly and clearly, adding intonation and variety to your voice as the grounding moves through its different stages.

• Finish with a clear instruction for everyone to open their eyes (if eyes were shut) and become fully present.

SUGGESTED WARM-UPS:

• **Physical:** Self introductions; ask each person to use the animal or plant they have come as to provide an activity for the whole circle to follow. For example, chickens hopping, trees in a storm, or whales breaching. You can turn this into a more elaborate game if you like by creating an action sequence. After the second person has demonstrated their activity, everyone repeats the second, and then the first person's activity. Once the third person has demonstrated their activity, the group repeats the third, second, and then first person's activity, and so on.

• **Vocal:** Sounding for light and dark; after introducing the idea of sounding (and having done some practice if needed), have the whole group create an extended sound for darkness, then one for light. Divide the group into two halves and have the dark and light sounds find a balance with each other. Play around with it!

3. Creating a Sacred Space

• **Cast a circle:** If you want to give your circle casting a spring flavor, this can be done with a circle of flowers or green leaves. Otherwise, have someone walk around the perimeter of your circle drawing the outline of the circle with their hand or a magical tool.

• **Call to the directions and the elements:** Have four people each calling to one of the quarters and all together to Above and Below. This can also be done by one person.

Northern Hemisphere:

East	Air	Birds, insects, creatures of air
South	Fire	Spirits, dragons, mythical beings, creatures of fire
West	Water	Fish, dolphins and whales, creatures of water
North	Earth	Animals, trees and plants, creatures of earth

Above and Below

Southern Hemisphere:

East	Air	Birds, insects, creatures of air
North	Fire	Spirits, dragons, mythical beings, creatures of fire
West	Water	Fish, dolphins and whales, creatures of water
South	Earth	Animals, trees and plants, creatures of earth

Above and Below

4. Introducing the Spring Equinox

Have one person explain the Spring Equinox. Include the information that it is one of the two days in the year (the two equinoxes) when light and dark are of equal length—halfway between the Summer and Winter Solstices. At the Spring Equinox, we swing into the light half of the Wheel of the Year.

Equinoxes are ideally placed for rituals of balance, of deliberately seeking to bring a balance where things have been out of balance. The Spring Equinox calls for outward balance in the world while at autumn the tides turn inward. Thus a ritual for peace and aligning with the earth is very appropriate. You might also like to include local information on how the Festival is relevant to what is happening where you are.

After the initial explanation, ask each person to contribute their own ideas about what the Spring Equinox or this time of year means to them. It may mean the final end to winter, a good time to be in the garden, or a time to begin new projects. If it is a large group (over twenty people), you can break into smaller groups for this section.

You may wish to include in the discussion the aspect of the Spring Equinox as a balancing time with relevance to real-life situations, such as emerging from a difficult or inward-focused time, seeking a balance between work and home, or trying to achieve a balanced understanding of a situation. Bringing the themes of the Festival closer to home and real life rather than abstract discussions of preparing and planting fields (particularly if you are not in a rural area) can be done in a second round of the sharing and will make the ritual much more immediate and relevant.

5. Learning the Chant

Introduce the chant or chants you will be using later in the ritual. There are many chants on CDs, online, and in songbooks. You may already have favorite chants that are well-known to your group. You might also have a songwriter among you. Choose a simple song or chant that is true to the themes of your ritual and teach it to the group by singing it a couple of times and then teaching it line by line. It's useful to sing it through together at least eight or ten times, so when you begin singing later in the ritual everyone can easily join in without being having to be reminded of the words or tune.

6A. Elemental Groups

Depending on how many and what ages children attending the ritual are, your ritual may look quite different from here on in. If your ritual is very child-oriented, use this piece of the ritual. If there are fewer, none, or mainly older children present, you can use Future Visions instead in 6B below.

Ask the group to divide into four elemental groups according to the costume they are wearing. Birds, insects, and creatures of the air should gather in the east. Whales, fish, and other creatures of water should gather in the west. Earth-bound animals and plants will be in the north in the Northern Hemisphere and in the south in the Southern Hemisphere. Any fire or magical creatures such as dragons, fairies, or phoenixes should gather in the south in the Northern Hemisphere and the north in the Southern Hemisphere. You may wish to divide your group slightly differently to get more evenly sized groups, for example warm-blooded animals may be in the fire quarter leaving plants and cold-blooded animals in the earth quarter.

Ask each group to create a small presentation of what their elemental grouping brings to the Peace Altar. This can be a song, a short play, a dance, or another offering. For example, the fire group may bring strong energy for creating change that they express in a powerful dance, or the water group may bring healing with a healing song. Allow the groups about twenty minutes to create their enactments, which should be about two to five minutes long. Each elemental group then enacts their presentation for the others.

6B. Future Visions

This is the alternative from 6A for groups that have mainly or all adults.

Each person is asked to represent the being they have come as, whether that be an earthworm, a sea hawk, a fairy, a daffodil, a bat, or any other creature they might be.

Begin with a dance where everyone is asked to embody their characters and move and dance as those beings. You can play a track of music for this or dance to drumming if you have drummers present.

Gather around the Peace Altar and have each being introduce themselves. For example, *I am dragonfly, and I live in the marshes and near rivers, I am cat and I like to prowl in forests and gardens, I am dragon and I live deep in the caves with my treasure,* or *I am dolphin and I love to play in the ocean.*

Explain that the group will create a collective future vision of the best possible future for the earth in one hundred years time. Say the year it will be in one hundred years. Then, asking everyone to close their eyes, speak a simple lead-in to help each person imagine this world of a hundred years in the future. Ask them to think of the elements (earth, fire, air, and water) and how those will be in this ideal future. Ask them to think of how the humans will be relating to the creatures and plants of this future world. Spend a moment in silence.

Then everyone opens their eyes and speaks one or two things they saw in their vision. For example, the bee may speak of how the bees have returned, and how clear and clean the air is. The oak may speak of trees being sacred, and of new groves that have been planted. The phoenix may speak of how the old fairy tales and songs have been remembered and are taught again.

Ask everyone to hold this collective vision clearly in their minds, and then announce now it is time to look not quite so far ahead, just ten years into the future. Say the year it will be in ten years. Ask everyone to close their eyes again, and imagine a future just ten years ahead that is heading toward that future of hundred years time. Ask them to think of the elements again (earth, fire, air, and water) and how those may be in this year ten years in the future. Ask them to think of how humans will be relating to the creatures and plants. Spend a moment in silence.

Then everyone opens their eyes and speaks one or two things they saw in their vision. For example, the koala may speak of corridors of gum trees being planted, and tunnels built under roads for them to cross safely from one feeding ground to another. The basil plant may speak of a growing understanding of the use of herbs and natural medicines. The salmon may speak of the rivers beginning to be cleaned up.

Ask everyone to hold this collective vision clearly in their minds, and then announce that now it is time to look just one year into the future. Say the year it will be in one year. Ask everyone to close their eyes again and imagine a future just one year ahead. Ask them to think of what achievements the next year will bring or what achievements may be begun. Ask them to think of the elements (earth, fire, air, and water) and what may change for the better in any element. Ask how each person may have changed by then. Ask them for any visions or words that come to them. Spend a moment in silence.

Then everyone opens their eyes and speaks one thing they saw in their vision. For example, the forest fairy may speak of a community tree planting, or the cat may talk of being kept inside at night, or the whale may talk of the seas becoming safer.

Then ask each person to think of one thing they can offer to this collective vision. One person may choose to make their household fully recycling, another person might commit to putting some regular hours into the community garden, and another might decide to speak to their workplace or school about visions for peace or sustainability. It's good to lead this section yourself, to set an example. After each person has spoken, they speak their words of peace that they brought with them.

7. Spring Egg Hunt

The activity of making painted eggs is fully described on page 113, immediately after the ritual.

Announce it is time for the Spring Egg Hunt. Each person is to go to the area where the eggs have been hidden and search for an egg. When they find an egg, ask them to pay careful attention to where it is. Explain there is just one decorated egg for each person (though you may have hidden a few extras) and if there are chocolate eggs as well, mention that.

After the Egg Hunt, come back together. Ask everyone what messages they receive from their egg (especially for the next six months, the light half of the year), from how the egg looks, where they found it, and what they feel about it. One person may feel their yellow egg decorated with flowers is telling them it's time to enjoy life; another may feel the egg they found hidden high up in the fork of a tree is telling them to look carefully, not everything you want is straight ahead of you; and someone who found an egg covered in red and pink hearts may be reminded that love is the most important thing to them.

8. Raising Energy

If you have a drummer or percussionist, this person can lead into the song. Start quietly reminding others of the words and tune and gradually increase the energy of the song. Turn it into a round if you like.

This is the time to raise energy if you choose. You may also choose to do a spiral dance, or a different dance.

9. Complete the Ritual

Acknowledge the directions and elements in the reverse order that they were called and dissolve the circle. Generally, the same people who did the calling and casting do this.

- **Acknowledge the directions and elements:**

Northern Hemisphere:
Below and Above

North	Earth	Animals, trees and plants, creatures of earth
West	Water	Fish, dolphins and whales, creatures of water
South	Fire	Spirits, dragons, mythical beings, creatures of fire
East	Air	Birds, insects, creatures of air

Southern Hemisphere:
Below and Above

South	Earth	Animals, trees and plants, creatures of earth
West	Water	Fish, dolphins and whales, creatures of water
North	Fire	Spirits, dragons, mythical beings, creatures of fire
East	Air	Birds, insects, creatures of air.

• **Dissolve the circle:** If a circle was cast, the same person walks around it in the opposite direction gathering up the energy or otherwise dispersing it. If you scattered flowers or leaves, you can sweep them up. If you were outside, they may already be lost in the grass or earth, but you could symbolically sweep or rake them away or else leave them as decoration and a reminder that a circle has been held there.

Thank each person for coming and for what they have contributed and begin your Spring Equinox Feast, if you are having one.

Spring Equinox Activity: Painted Eggs

You can make Spring Equinox Eggs in preparation for larger ritual, to carry out a traditional Easter hunt, or just to have them on the altar at this time of the year. Usually everyone likes other people's eggs better than their own—and in this process you end up with someone else's egg! This activity is not just for children, and a surprising number of the eggs turn into beautiful art objects.

Paint the eggs a day or so before you want to use them as they can take a while to dry. Don't put them in the refrigerator once you've begun working on them; the paint destabilizes and goes sticky. Once they've been out of the fridge for a while we don't usually eat our eggs, but use them as decorations.

You will need:
- At least 2 hard-boiled eggs per person. If you start with 3 each, it allows for some breakages and also means you can move on to painting another while one egg is drying

- 1 eggcup per egg. Either use proper eggcups or pieces of an egg carton. A little bit of paper wadded into the bottom of the cup means the egg sits up higher and you can paint the middle as well as the top

- Paints; tubes of strongly colored water paints or inks, colored markers, etc

- Usual paint tools, such as rinsing water, newspaper to protect your work surface, and something to mix paint colors on

- Tiny paint brushes and toothpicks for fine detail

- Craft glue

- A few decorations such as sequins, feathers, narrow ribbon, and glitter

- Camera (optional)

Time:
- At least an hour

Intention

Your intention may be as simple as celebrating spring, nature, magic, or creativity; or you may have a more focused intent, such as growing beyond old limitations. Decide on your intention before you begin painting the eggs. If you are doing this activity with children, spend a few moments to assist them by asking what ideas they get from the intention—colors, shapes, and feelings.

Method

Hard-boil the eggs in heavily salted water on a gentle boil. Start with a few more than you need (you won't be able to use broken eggs, although of course you can eat them). I've always used hen's eggs (organic and free range), but you could use smaller or larger eggs.

Remember that eggs, even hard-boiled ones, break easily. It's easy to end up with paint all over your hands and blotches all over your eggs; it's also easy to drop an egg on the floor. Paint takes a while to dry, so work on one half of each egg (top or bottom) and then leave it to dry; this is much easier than trying to paint the whole egg in one go, with no way to hold on to it properly or rest it to dry.

I like to paint each of my eggs differently. I might have a night sky egg, a spring flowers egg, and a spiral-with-dots egg. It would also be beautiful to have them the same, or similar. Eggs have quite a small surface area, so it's the detail of it rather than the expanse of the eggs that makes egg-painting a time-consuming project. If you have young children, you might settle for them painting just one egg each, and you may have to spend a lot of time helping them. Eggs often evolve through the painting process, becoming more complex than originally imagined.

- You may like to cast a circle, sing a song, or bless the eggs before beginning.

- Explain what these eggs will be used for (a later ritual, or to take home, or to give to each other).

- You may like to either talk a little about the Spring Equinox or have each person say a few words about what it means to them. You can also talk about the tradition of eggs at this time of the year; traditionally they are painted red as fertility blessings.

- Introduce your intention if you have one, as discussed on the previous page, or suggest some possible intentions for individuals. Give out a few pointers about the process of painting eggs and the materials you have.

- Begin painting! Painting a base color is a good way to start, and after it dries you can paint more elaborate decorations on it, but not everyone likes to do this. With children especially, try to paint the egg while it is actually in the egg cup.

- Paint half to two-thirds of the way down the egg, then let it dry before you turn it over and paint the other part. Meanwhile you can work on a different egg, help someone else, or have a break.

- Once the eggs are fully painted you can add decorations; sprinkle glitter onto wet paint; or glue a few tiny feathers, sequins, or a narrow ribbon to your egg once the paint is dry. If you have thin, clear-drying glue, you can get a shiny effect from painting it on the finished egg.

- I like to take a photo of all the eggs together before they are given away or used in a ritual.

Beltaine

*Celebrated on May 1 in the Northern Hemisphere
and November 1 in the Southern Hemisphere.*

Beltaine

Everyone who was present remembers the first Beltaine we asked the children to become a pack of hounds. The idea was to enact a hunt with a man as the quarry. Whoever was caught would become the Beltaine God, the Horned Lord. It was a sunny afternoon. We thought the children would appreciate a romp on the grass and the men would oblige them.

We were on a rural property and from the back veranda a pleasantly grassed slope led broadly down toward a valley. To one side of the house the ground dropped steeply, uneven with rock and weeds into a little twisting gully which was thick with awkward saplings. There were about seven children, ranging between the ages of five and twelve. Giving the instructions I couldn't really tell if they were paying much attention, but I trusted that it would work out.

The men jogged off down the gentle slope, all except one who headed for the steep hill, picking his way carefully down. I'd planned to have the children wait a moment, giving the men a head start, but there was no holding them back. They leapt off the veranda and charged as a group straight downhill through the weeds and rocks of the steep incline. They shrieked. They leapt and tumbled. The man they were chasing looked back and picked up his pace, and the children practically fell down the hill, shouting and spreading out and they'd become hounds like I'd asked them. They were ferocious; they tore after their quarry as he began dodging along the bottom of the gully, in and out of small trees. The rest of the men stopped still on their nice grassy slope, and on the veranda we held our breaths, expecting a twisted ankle at the very least, and perhaps concussion or a broken leg. We had shouted, *Not that way!* after the children the instant they headed for the steep hill, but of course that didn't stop them. They were hounds, they had a quarry who'd chosen unstable ground, and they were after him.

It was a great shifting into the mythic that we watched, slightly horrified, as the human veneer tore off our children and they hunted in a fast, enthusiastic, jumbled, and killing way. They wouldn't have cared if one or two of them were injured, they were in the thrill of it. We'd asked them to throw away all the usual, sensible boundaries and become animal, and they did almost instinctively and without question. Damon was one of those children who tumbled down that hill. Normally a physically timid child, there was no sign of that in the hound energy, the pack energy they'd sourced, instantly it seemed, from collective cultural knowledge. None of them had ever seen a pack of hounds.

They shouted to each other, *Over here! You go that way! Grab him!* and I felt we'd slid back to some alternate time or culture, perhaps one where stoning was permitted, or rough justice metered out to criminals, misfits, or the unlucky. You could see they wanted to take a bite or two out of him, getting him onto the ground. He was brought back dusty, panting and a little bruised. The children were children again. The men seemed bemused that the whole thing hadn't been more fun, but the women, who'd seen it from the vantage point of the veranda, were shaken.

That was a long time ago, that ritual, but it set the pattern of our Beltaine gatherings. We did run the Wild Hunt in following years—of course the children adored it—but ever afterward we ran it cautiously with specific areas the hunt was allowed to run within and an adult hounds master with a whistle and some basic hound training. That readiness of the children to leap raw into the animal showed what I discovered about Beltaine again and again whenever I looked: that Beltaine is not pretty, not nice; it is strong and wild and somewhat bloody.

Beltaine Memoir

I call to the Goddess as she rises out of the sea and her consort, the stag, descending the rocky path down to her hidden beach! Cathryn cries out, facing the Cross-Quarter of Imbolc. *I call to the place where the river meets the sea, flowing in and out with the tides, where the salt water mixes with the fresh water,* intones Trinda, in the Cross-Quarter of Beltaine. *To the elemental workings of this ancient volcano that carved out this land we live on!* shouts Glenn in the Lammas Cross-Quarter. And I take this blazing circle, made of the vibrant, ferocious Cross-Quarters and ground it into the final place, Samhain. *I call to the mysteries and the ancient circles! I call through the veils and I call to the Northern Hemisphere, celebrating Samhain on this day.* We all turn to face the center and Damon finishes, *I call Below, to the rainbow serpent who dreams the land, and Above, to the stars!*

Beltaine has begun. It's one of our favorite Festivals; from year to year we elaborate on the ritual, but we don't often rewrite it from scratch. It's too well loved. Last year's God is dressed in the antlers of the stag, a gold-painted, forked, and many-twigged branch. We gather the children together as a pack of hounds under a hounds master and train them to the whistle. It's a smaller pack than other years, only about eight of them. They are restless, they're growing up, but they're still keen to hunt.

Paul is young and fit as the old God; he makes a good run down the field and along the side of the lantana; I can see him calculating his moves, plotting his trajectory as the kids pelt after him. He cuts left, planning to run down the hill and around to the back of the house when suddenly Damon leaps out from the pack in a flying football tackle and grabs his legs and they both crash to the ground. It's impressive, though I see raised eyebrows and winces among the watchers as we think of broken teeth and cracked jaws.

Paul is brought back for the challenges, winded and panting, clearly not in as good condition as he was fifteen minutes ago. Anyone can challenge him for the position of the God and whoever wins the final of three challenges will be the Beltaine God for this year. The challenges are written on red, green, and yellow cards and each comes with three parts: Spirit, Skill, and Strength. Glenn steps forward to face Paul, choosing the green card. To replace Paul he has to win two parts of it. The Spirit challenge on the green card is prayer.

Glenn gazes at the sky, opens his arms and speaks a prayer for the birds. He talks of their beauty, how they call us to freedom and how they remind us of our own spirit. When it's Paul's turn, he looks down at the earth. He's not nearly so comfortable speaking, it doesn't come across as poetic, but he says, again and again, *the earth, the earth*, and his voice breaks a little as if he's speaking to a lover, and we are all moved and decide he's the winner.

The Skill of the green card is archery. There's a target set up in the driveway, and Damon bustles about with the bow and arrows, giving instructions. We all stand back, wishing them luck as they fire three arrows. Paul tries his best, but his arrows fall short, while Glenn manages to get a couple of arrows into the target and is declared the winner.

The challenge for Strength is balancing, so Paul and Glenn each stand on one leg. Paul spreads his arms out, but Glenn concentrates everything downward into the ground, as if he was immovable, and eventually Paul topples and Glenn has won.

Damon steps forward. The challenges have always been something he's loved, and this year I wrote them without his help, knowing he wanted to win. He's challenged for the God before but never won because of his size; he drew a wrestling challenge against a grown man last year. I imagined them as stags or horses, challenging for leadership and the young ones being knocked back, taught their place year after year while they gradually gain strength and experience. I don't really like the children to challenge, but I see the imperative of it; you can never win from the sidelines, and never win without losing first, if you're young. Damon's only thirteen and I want to snatch him back and keep him safe a few more years.

This time there's an added charge, because Glenn is his father. Damon chooses the yellow card and I read out the Spirit challenge: invocation. The challenger, Damon, goes first, launching immediately into *Tir-na-nog*, a delicate and wistful poem about the hidden land of faerie. He has spoken and practiced it so many times; I know every lift of tone and have discussed each pause and emphasis with him, so I hear it in my head as well as in his voice, strengthening with this recital, Damon claiming the words of the author as his own. It's beautiful and people are impressed with his recitation—his memory, confidence, and expression—but I sense its weakness; this poem is the voice of a lost soul, yearning after the impossible—the opposite of a victor.

Glenn replies, beginning the much more powerful *Taliesin,* an invocation of magical, bardic powers, and I expect him to win. He is still the mature one, worldly and experienced compared with Damon's childishness. But a few lines in he stumbles, forgetting the words. Damon knows this poem as well and whispers Glenn a prompt of the next line. He's proud of his dad, ready to challenge him but not minding if he wins, if he proves he's still the stronger one. Glenn picks up the line with a grateful look at Damon and continues, but then stops again. Damon speaks the next line loudly and then Glenn grinds to a halt, shaking his head and stopping entirely. Damon steps forward and continues the poem, speaking it through to the end. So he's recited not just his own poem, but Glenn's as well, and what can we say? He's won, easily.

I look at their faces, my child and his father. They are both raw, taken aback by what is happening between them, and in front of an audience. Damon's face is shifting between disbelief, eagerness, and uncertainty. He's held between his determination and his love for his father. Glenn is undone in his own lack of preparation. He thinks holding the God would be nice. For Damon, holding the God is a great, emblematic moment, urging him on, and it's only now in the middle of it that Glenn becomes aware of Damon's yearning, Glenn's own lack of intensity catching him off guard before that continual pressing, year after year as Damon gets taller, stronger, luckier until it's enough, finally, for the old to be forced to give way before it.

The Skill of the yellow card is creativity and after a brief discussion, we give them five minutes to each construct an altar. Glenn displays to us a beautiful tableau, a young woman as the Goddess and other women kneeling around her. But Damon sits on the grass with the smallest child there and plays with her, constructing a tiny altar with a few leaves and miniature flowers between them. It is so simple, a boy on the verge of adolescence playing with a three-year-old girl, bending his head down to talk to her, helping her hands arrange their flowers. They don't look at us, but there's no contest and he wins without protest. He's almost trembling as he stands; he's won already.

But Glenn won't let it stop at that and you can imagine the king horse, the head stag refusing to be beaten even when it's obvious. He's defeated, but he's still got another fight left in him. For Strength the challenge is handstands, and Glenn, with years of practice, does win. Perhaps it helps him retain his pride, when Damon replaces him in the center. And then no one stands forward to take the Red card. Perhaps they don't want to take this victory away from him, or perhaps it isn't rising so strong in them, the need for it, and so Damon is declared this year's God and the antlers affixed to him. Someone rushes down to the house for a stool, since he's not very tall and traditionally we turn the man who's won into the Maypole.

Trinda's written a song for the Maypole dance.

Round and round and round and round
Reach the sky and touch the ground
Up and down and in and out
THIS is what my song's about!

We tie our ribbons onto a red chest-band bound around Damon and whisper our spells to him, wishes for love, healing, for a baby, or for good luck. Then we stand back, holding our ribbons and begin the dance, weaving in and out of each other around the pivot point of Damon, standing blazing and immobile on the stool, his arms up and golden antlers on his head. My life's been pivoting around him for thirteen years. I'm not ready to release him into the world, but this is a foreshadowing, and I don't have any other children, he's the only one. I feel like Ishtar binding her son to the tree; celebrating and mourning at the same time.

We're singing as we're dancing, and every time we get to the word *THIS* in the chant, we shout out LOVE or JOY or LIFE or whatever we want, changing and weaving the words and our spells as we weave our ribbons round my son in spirals of color. When the ribbons are finished we stand back in a wide circle, gazing at our God, young but wearing the antlers already, encased in spelled ribbons, and we shout out our spells, all at once. He's too grave to smile; I don't know what he's feeling.

We release the circle and go into the house for our feast. Someone painstakingly cuts the ribbons off Damon, binding them into little bundles for people to take home for their altars or love spells. Beltaine is made up of the unexpected, that's where its power is—the sudden rearrangements, the release of desire, the permission of wildness. The push and pull of sexual energy, of invading and relenting, of beckoning and response. Sometimes on Beltaine a lover has come to me, when I thought I had none; one year I danced wildly and flirted behind my mask with three men but went home alone, happily. Last year at Beltaine I ended a relationship.

When I watched Damon and Glenn in their confrontation, what shocked me was that I had no place in it. Does a mother's allegiance switch from the old to the new, when her son's old enough to defeat his father? The mares don't follow their old lord when the young one wins, the doe doesn't run off with last year's stag, who can protect her no longer. They turn to the victor, who is young and strong. Of course my allegiance is with Damon, this youthful, blossoming being, and one who implements so perfectly everything I've taught him, even to stepping beyond that. I watched a change take place when he won, I felt it in myself. I grew a little older, moved a bit further around the Wheel. Beltaine by Beltaine I am moving on to the outer edges of fertility and sexual love. I don't have a lover. I have my son, growing and striving to become a man, and it makes me older. Beltaine's essence is change, and it's never what you expect.

Celebration of the Wild

Beltaine's about sex, not love, my eighteen-year-old son reminded me irritably as we sat down to plan. *Let's keep the ritual to what it's actually about.* It was a good reminder. We tend to get all hearts-and-flowers about Beltaine, when it's really about fertility and reproductive sex. If you lived in rural Europe anytime before industrialization, Beltaine would have been when food became more plentiful and all of nature burst forth. It's about sap running through the veins of the trees and wild animals rutting; it's a fire festival of celebration and license in a time of year freed from the scarcities and ferocity of winter.

On the Wheel of the Year, Beltaine is directly opposite Samhain, the festival that honors death. Between the Northern and Southern Hemispheres, these Festivals of sex and death are celebrated simultaneously, twice a year. And they are the Festivals whose Pagan elements have most successfully survived, as May Day and Halloween, uncorrupted by Christian interpretations—unlike how much of the symbolism of the Spring Equinox has been subsumed into Easter celebrations and the Winter Solstice into Christmas.

Beltaine and Samhain are the Festivals everyone loves most. There is reliably a far bigger turnout for those rituals than any other. Even in our modern life they're still seen as celebrations where it's permissible to break the boundaries. Somehow on those days, sex in the fields, flirting with strangers, or dashing around the streets in a cloak and mask are condoned. Children especially love them. They're given license to run a little bit mad, becoming hounds or hobgoblins and working as a pack to torment adults. We don't tend to associate children with either sex or death, but in fact they're very at home in the rawness of these events. If you think about it, children are still quite closely tied in with the edges of sex and death that are attendant on birth.

In England I saw Morris dancers, traditionally associated with Beltaine. This troop had men in their sixties (and older) and a small number who looked to be in their late teens or early twenties. After the dance a young Asian woman asked me what it meant and I tried to explain. Morris dancers are all men because they come as lovers to the Goddess, the earth. They've got bells on their legs and stamp the ground to wake her up. Their dance is about sex and fertilizing the earth. She looked startled and moved backward, but listening to my stumbling description was one of the older Morris dancers and he nodded. *That's right*, he said, *that's what we do.* I was thrilled he agreed, because I hadn't been certain Morris dancers thought about it that way.

The young woman looked even more unsettled, murmured some excuse and left. I asked the dancer about the obvious age gap in his troop. He told me that Morris dancing is passed down in families but neither his son nor the sons of his contemporaries had been interested, and they thought maybe it would die out. But then some of their grandsons began asking to be taught the dances, and so it seemed it would continue, after all. He was prosaic, but I felt like crying with the turning of it, the slenderness of survival and yet, how robust it was now, this mix of generations—the young and the old together, made more poignant by the missing generation. As if there'd been a war and all the men of a certain age were gone.

Beltaine corresponds to the stage in life where we're expected to choose a partner, settle down, and reproduce. Of course that carries its own surprises as we get pregnant unexpectedly, or by the wrong person, or we can't get pregnant when we want. Some of us flout convention in matters of partners, sexuality, and career choice. We are queer, gay, multi-partnered, or remain stubbornly single. We may abandon a conventional career path, or never have one. Some of us remain or become adventurers, artists, or spiritual seekers instead of accountants, teachers, and tradespeople. In fact, it is these twists that carry our fate, and may determine our life course, at least for the next while, far more potently than those conventional expectations did.

Beltaine can also be aligned with times where passion carries the day. We abandon that university course to go traveling in South America, change careers in midlife, or become more active and adventurous in retirement than we ever were while working and raising a family. These changes are not made logically by watching investments and calculating returns. These changes are made from the heart, inspired, desperate, impassioned, and (to those looking on) sometimes almost random. Beltaine energy is in the folk song where the lady leaves her castle to go with her gypsy lover, it's in the woman who has a child on her own at forty, it's in someone deciding to live their true sexuality after a lifetime of repression.

Beltaine carries elements of the wild and of randomness. There are rumors that on this one night the rigid rules of society were loosened and you could, in the dark, lie with anyone. And if it happened that a couple had been infertile, but on this night the woman conceived, well, that was a blessing. Fertility festivals might facilitate survival of the fittest, where the most attractive partners get extra chances to generate offspring, but there's a whole lot of guesswork, randomness, and surprises along the way. The Maypole dance itself demonstrates this, bringing you face to face with so many different, possible partners, but only exactly half of those who are dancing—the other half you never meet at all.

Even the idea of a May Queen (and perhaps our modern, contentious beauty pageants follow on from this tradition) has a random element to it. Today she was chosen, but next year it will be another and so on and on. Often our way of choosing someone to play the God or Goddess in a ritual echoes this randomness; the short straw, the closest birth date, the one picked by a blindfolded child, or the one caught in the chase. And fertility itself is like this; it was this ovum, on this month fertilized; not this other one, or this one, or this, or this. I have only one child, but how many eggs have I released over my fertile years? Two hundred or more. And as for sperm, between twenty million and three hundred million are released at one time. So what are the chances of Damon, this exact being, coming into existence?

Beltaine prompts questions around the mystery of sexual attraction. It's *opposites attract* or perhaps we all end up with someone born no more than two suburbs away, or we find familiarity in a face, or fall in love with someone whose strengths match our weaknesses ... Sexual attraction doesn't follow any rules or we'd surely have worked them out by now. Well, biologically perhaps there are some rules.

Apparently a woman is much, much more likely to have sex with a new lover when she's fertile (Bellis, M. A., and R. R. Baker. 1990. "Do Females Promote Sperm Competition?: Data for Humans." *Animal Behavior.* 40: 997–99). Since most women don't know when they're fertile, it must be largely unconscious and surely at least partially driven by biology or hormones. Whether it's the start of a relationship or a single occurrence, that self-generated fertility drug has a say in our actions. And perhaps we can understand that drive, thinking of small, isolated communities with a strong possibility of inbreeding; then along comes a traveler—a soldier, adventurer, merchant, minstrel—and his genes will help that whole village or tribe. And so maybe the girl he chooses isn't the prettiest, or the one he'd have the best conversation with or the one he'd marry; maybe she's just the one who's fertile on that particular night.

Beltaine and the license of Beltaine give us a few extra degrees of freedom. Perhaps we dress sexily for a Beltaine Ball, or our wish at the Maypole is for a baby, a lover, or a change and we don't care so much about the fine points right that moment. And in the strength of Beltaine we might be granted it—here's a lover, a baby, or something that will change your life—to think back on our own actions a few months later and wonder, what came over me? Was that the sap rising in the trees? The buds coming into flower? Was that the deer rutting, the birds nesting? Those acts of sex, of seduction and…was that me? And if it's left you with the difficulties of a lover you'd never normally choose, or a baby not in the most perfect circumstances, or a surprise career shift, Beltaine has still been served.

Sexuality is wild. It's not about maintaining the borders of civilization, except and only at the point of keeping them populated. Marriage, mortgage payments, child maintenance, and family planning are about those borders, those rules and strictures. But sexuality isn't. Talk with people about their sexuality, its history, and the quirks, peculiarities, and fluctuations, or examine your own sexuality with deep honesty, and you won't find any rules. Fears, maybe. Cultural avoidances, for sure. Habits, certainly. But actual hard-and-fast rules? I think not. Even the rule of fertility requiring strict heterosexuality is overturned; it is when sexuality is essentially wild and uncontained that fertility is most enhanced. Fertility—if that is the Beltaine force—may inspire dancing with a dozen partners, flirting with everyone, and sleeping with someone other than our normal lover. But it's not about boundaries or rules; it's truly random.

Sexuality is the life force that threads through our veins with the beating of our hearts. It's in the threads of connection we toss to strangers. It's in our dancing and singing and creativity. It responds when we put on (or take off) certain clothes, when we eat certain foods or our senses pick up different stimuli. It's something we can feel within ourselves when no one else is around, something we can share with a partner and a force we can acknowledge as present within friendships, communities, and in spiritual practice. Sexuality seems, of its essence, to be broad, diverse, and changeable. It results in connections between people, powerful emotions, creative inspirations, bonding, and sometimes in babies.

Sex is a natural force, akin to the power of the waterfall thundering into the pool, the tossing waves of the sea, or the wind singing among and bending the tree tops. We see it in nature endlessly, the interaction of one element with another, sighting birds in updrafts over cliffs and moist soil sprouting new plants. At Beltaine we join with the natural world in celebrating the raw appetite for life that is sometimes called lust, perhaps a little more wildly than at other times of the year, bursting forth with the season's energy. We hunt down the old God, dance the Maypole, and give gifts to strangers. Beltaine is a fertility Festival. It's about sex.

Beltaine Ritual

This ritual was written by Damon, Kellie, and Jane.

Notes: "Ritual Basics" on page 295 covers many aspects of ritual, including grounding, casting circles, invocations, and participation.

How to make Beltaine Charms to tie onto Maypole ribbons is described on page 147.

Section 8, "The Maypole Dance," is the central part of this ritual.

Ask everyone to bring:

- A ribbon for those who wish to dance the Maypole (small children can share with a parent). Work out how long your ribbon needs to be for the height of your Maypole, remembering it wraps around and around the pole; 7–9 yards (6–8 meters) is a standard length

- Three tiny gifts (for example, a shell, a poem, and a flower)

- Food for the Beltaine Feast, if you are having one

Other things needed for this ritual:

- A Maypole. For many years we used a man for our Maypole; more conventionally, you can use a pole in the ground with a ring for the ribbons to be tied to, which is then raised to the top and fixed there

- A gong or chime to get people's attention at different stages in the ritual

- Drum/percussion instrument (one or more)

Clothing suggestion:

- Red, pink, white, and green

Roles in ritual:

These can all be done by different people or one or two people can take all or most of the roles depending on how confident and experienced the group is:

- Casting the circle and calling directions, which can be done by several different people or all by one person

- Grounding

- Leading warm-ups

- Invocations to invoke the Lord/Horned God and Lady/Earth Goddess, done by two people

- Two people to appear as the Lord/Horned God and the Lady/Earth Goddess; these can be the same as the people who invoked them

- Leading ritual and giving instructions (this role can be split among several people or kept to one person)

- Spiral dance leader

- Timekeeper (this may not be necessary, or can be combined with another role)

- Drummer/song leader

Length of Ritual: 1.5–2 hours

Ritual

1. Gathering

Welcome the group to the ritual space and take care of any housekeeping. If some people are unfamiliar with ritual etiquette, briefly explain how you'd like the ritual to run.

Announce the intention of the ritual. For example, *Today we honor Beltaine, ancient Festival of fertility, The intention of this ritual is to celebrate our passions and creativity*, or *We come together to reconnect with the earth in sacred ritual.*

Ask everyone to introduce themselves briefly. Start with yourself, to give a demonstration of the type of introduction you want. If you have a large group (over twenty), you can ask people simply to introduce themselves to the person or people next to them.

2. Grounding and Warm-ups

Warm-ups are optional, but great in a group that doesn't know each other well or isn't practiced in ritual, and also in groups with children.

GROUNDING:

- Briefly introduce the idea of grounding; explain that it is done to assist everyone to become more present, feel alive in their bodies, and release any distractions.

- Offer a seasonal grounding, asking people to become trees with the sap warming and running through them, to feel their leaves sprouting and growing. Ask them to feel the life force flooding in from the increasing sunlight, and the rich nutrients fed to them by the earth.

- Speak slowly and clearly, adding emotion and shadings to your description.

- Finish with a clear instruction for everyone to open their eyes (if they were shut) and become fully present.

SUGGESTED WARM-UPS:
- **Physical:** Weaving bodies; learn a circle dance or a strip-the-willow dance that requires weaving in and out of other people.

- **Vocal:** Stretching voices; try a variety of vocal warm-up exercises as a group, including running your voices up and down the full reach of your range, and changing your sound from loud to soft to very loud again. If someone in the group is a singer, ask them to lead a few more.

3. Creating a Sacred Space
- **Cast a circle:** If you want to give your circle casting a particularly Beltaine flavor, this can be done by adding singing and flourishes to the normal circle cast of having someone walk around the perimeter of your circle using their hand or a magical tool to draw the outline of the circle.

- **Call to the directions:** If you have a large gathering, call into eight directions and Above and Below. If you have a smaller group, you may choose to call just into the four Cross-Quarters, as Beltaine is a Cross-Quarter Festival. All together call Above and Below.

  Northern Hemisphere:

Northeast	Beginnings, dawn, the first flush of warmth
East	Growth, spring, the time of greening, promise
Southeast	Beltaine, passion, creativity, fertility
South	Heat, promise fulfilled, summer, love and union
Southwest	Harvest, realizations, letting go
West	Balance, autumn, gathering in
Northwest	Initiation, the spirits, other realms
North	Death and birth, winter, completion, and return

  Above and Below

Southern Hemisphere:

Southeast   Beginnings, dawn, the first flush of warmth

East   Growth, spring, the time of greening, promise

Northeast   Beltaine, passion, creativity, fertility

North   Heat, promise fulfilled, summer, love and union

Northwest   Harvest, realizations, letting go

West   Balance, autumn, gathering in

Southwest   Initiation, the spirits, other realms

South   Death and birth, winter, completion, and return

Above and Below

- **Invocations:** For Beltaine, it's lovely to have the two invited deities (male and female) dressed up and appear as the invocations begin or to make the invocations themselves. Invoke the fertile, passionate feminine and the wild, potent masculine.

4. Introducing Beltaine

Have one person stand forward and talk about Beltaine. Explain where it fits into the Wheel of the Year and how the Cross-Quarters are often considered more important seasonally than the equinoxes and solstices.

Beltaine is the Festival opposite to and balancing Samhain; the powerful themes of sex, fertility, and death are begun here to be picked up and completed in Samhain. It is also very much a season of flowering and fertility, sap rising, sensuality, and sexuality. You might also like to include local information relevant to Beltaine.

After the initial explanation, ask each person to contribute their own ideas about what Beltaine or this time of year means to them. It may mean flowers in the garden, a busy season at work, or the promise of summer coming. If it is a large group (over twenty people), you can break into smaller groups for this section.

You may wish to include in the discussion the idea of Beltaine as a time of fertility relevant to real-life situations, such as spending time with or searching for a lover, focusing on babies, or fertile creativity. Bringing the themes of the Wheel of the Year closer to home can be done in a second round of the sharing and makes the ritual much more immediate.

5. Learning the Chants

Introduce the chants you will be using later in the ritual. It's best to have more than one, as when the Maypole dancing goes on for a long time the same chant can get boring. It's good to also have a different song for the spiral dance.

There are many chants on CDs, online, and in songbooks. You may also have favorite chants that are known to your group or a songwriter among you. Choose simple songs or chants that are true to the themes of your ritual and teach each one to the group by singing it a couple of times and then teaching it line by line. It's useful to sing it through together at least eight or ten times so when you begin singing later everyone can easily join in without being having to be retaught the words or the tune.

6. Three Tiny Gifts Process

Ask everyone to have three tiny gifts ready; explain the process. The emphasis of this part of the ritual is on giving, not receiving. You may receive one, none, or many gifts, but the point is in the giving of your own three gifts. Each gift is to be given to a different person and gifts cannot be exchanged (meaning if someone gives you a gift, you cannot give them one in return). Usually, but not always, people explain why they have chosen that person to give their gift to. Mention you will use chimes (or whatever you have) to announce the ending of each round.

Announce the first gift is to be given to someone who represents something you are grateful for in your life. If you are grateful for your child, for example, you could give your gift to your child, or to any child. Allow a few minutes for this gifting to happen and then sound the chimes to signal it's time for the second gift.

Announce the second gift is to be given to someone who represents something you wish to draw into your life. For example if you wish to draw a woman friend into your life, you could give it to a woman you think may become a friend, or to any woman. Allow a few minutes for this gifting to happen and then sound the chimes to signal it's time for the third gift.

Announce the third gift is to be given to someone who represents something you admire or love. For example, if you admire your partner's courage, you could give your partner the gift, or anyone else who you sense or know has courage. Allow a few minutes for this to happen and then sound your chimes to signal this part of the ritual is finished.

7. The Maypole Dance

If you wish to tie Beltaine Ccharms onto your ribbons, instructions for making them are on page 147, immediately after the ritual.

A Maypole dance must have an even number of dancers.

Have people tie their ribbons to the Maypole ring, which is then lifted to the top (fix them on a band around the man's chest, if you are dancing around a man) and then stand back several meters, holding the ribbons, and facing a partner. Give all the instructions, practice the weaving movement a couple of times, and reintroduce the song before beginning the dance.

If dancing the Maypole has specific intention, whether it be either a group intention or individual intentions, remind the dancers of this before they begin. If the chant you are dancing with is about love, for instance, that may obviously be the intention.

For the dance, people stand facing each other in pairs, their left or right shoulder turned to the Maypole. Whichever way they are facing in this pairing, that is the way they will be facing for the entire dance.

Have all the people with their right shoulder turned to the Maypole take a step inward toward the Maypole, and all the people with their left shoulder to the Maypole take a step outward (they should still be looking at their partner). Those on the outside ring lift their ribbons high and take a few steps forward around the circle (counterclockwise), and those on the inside ring take a few steps forward (clockwise) and underneath the ribbon of their partner.

Each person is now facing a new partner. Those who were on the inside ring take a step outward and those on the outside ring step inward; although everyone is still facing the same direction they were before, the outside ring has become the inside ring, and the inside ring is now the outside ring. The people on the outside ring raise their ribbons and take a few steps forward around the circle; the people on the inside ring take a few steps forward underneath the raised ribbon (each person continuing in the same direction, but doing the opposite of what they did the first time). Everyone is now facing a new partner and once again they move inward or outward in turn.

This is the weaving motion of the dance, that every second person you pass, you pass on the outside, lifting your ribbon over them. The ribbons need to be kept taut throughout and will gradually weave their pattern down the Maypole, pulling the dancers in closer and closer as the ribbons get shorter. The pattern shows up much more clearly on a pole than it does when woven around a person. When the ribbons have run out at the end of the dance, you can hold hands around the Maypole and sing the chant through one last time or raise energy together.

It's great to have a few people not dancing who can drum and sing strongly. They can also decide when to introduce a different chant. Small children who want to be included can dance with a parent, holding onto the outside end of the ribbon but staying close.

If you've woven your ribbons around someone, you will need to carefully cut them off after the dance. The ribbons can then be made into little Beltaine bundles and taken home for good luck. If you wove them around a pole, they can stay there until next year when you can unwind them, cut them off, or simply weave a new layer of ribbons over the top.

8. Personal Passions and Passions for the Earth

This section functions as a lead-in to the spiral dance, which completes the ritual. To rouse the passions of the participants, a powerful, gospel-style delivery of the questions is ideal, and the answers come from everyone at once. To help people get a feel for this, have a bit of practice with question-and-answer delivery, with a caller in the center calling out a question and encouraging everyone to shout back, *Yes!* a few times. For example, *Are you ready now to declare your passions? Can you tell me any louder? Do you know what your passions are? Will you shout them out to let the wind take them? Will you send them out into the world?*

Then the caller shouts out the questions: *What are you passionate about? What's your passion in your own life? What's your passion for this community? What's your passion for the earth?* The caller waits between each one for everyone to shout back their answers (all at once). Immediately after this is done, move into the spiral dance. It's best if a few people know in advance about this transition and are ready to set the example of what to do.

9. Spiral Dance

The leader of the dance should have either done this before or practiced a few times.

You can begin as a circle holding hands or in a line of people holding hands that continues to grow as people join in. Start slowly, moving in time with the chant (use a different chant than the one you sang with the Maypole). You can have one or several people drumming.

The leader of the spiral dance heads in the direction of the sun (clockwise in the Northern Hemisphere, counterclockwise in the Southern Hemisphere). The leader spirals slowly in toward the center, bringing the long body of the snake of people behind before turning outward. Any switchback turn should bring you face-to-face with the dancer following you.

There are two ways to do this dance. In either case, drummers can be in the center or off to the side.

In the first method, the leader can spiral quite tightly all the way into the center before doing a switchback turn and heading outward between the coils that have been created by the line of people; the leader will be dancing around and around until the whole circle is unwound again (and in the process meeting every person face to face), finishing up back in a big circle (facing outward). At the end, everyone drops hands and turns to face the center and raises energy in a big whoosh or an extended high tone.

In the second method, the leader spirals into the center about one and a half turns around the circle then does the switchback turn and heads outward; once all the way out, the leader does another switchback turn and heads inward again. This time the leader spirals tightly all the way in and when everyone is wrapped around the center as close as they can get, hands are dropped and a toning begins to raise and eventually release energy.

10. Complete the Ritual

Honor and thank all those invoked, acknowledge the directions in the reverse order that they were called, and dissolve the circle. Generally the same people who did the invoking, calling, and casting do this.

- **Acknowledge:** Offer thanks and honoring to the aspects of the God and Goddess who were invoked at the beginning of the ritual.

- **Acknowledge the directions:**

  Northern Hemisphere:
  Below and Above

North	Place of rest and rebirth
Northwest	Spirits, other realms
West	Balance, autumn, harvest
Southwest	Brilliance and sacrifice
South	Coming summer, love, and union
Southeast	Beltaine, passion, creativity, and fertility
East	Spring, the time just passed that will come again
Northeast	Always beginning

  Southern Hemisphere:
  Below and Above

South	Place of rest and rebirth
Southwest	Spirits, other realms
West	Balance, autumn, harvest
Northwest	Brilliance and sacrifice

North   Coming summer, love, and union
Northeast   Beltaine, passion, creativity, and fertility
East   Spring, the time just passed that will come again
Southeast   Always beginning

- **Dissolve the circle:** If a circle was cast, the same person walks around it in the opposite direction, gathering up the energy or otherwise dispersing it.

Thank each person for coming and for what they have contributed and begin your Beltaine Feast, if you are having one.

Beltaine Activity: Charms

You can make Beltaine charms on their own or to use in a larger ritual; sometimes I've strung them onto the ribbons that weave the Maypole or I've tied them onto the Maypole at the end. Alternatively, you can tie them onto a flowering bush, place them on your altar, place them under your pillow, or give them away. Make them with a group, with your family, friends, or by yourself.

To make the charms, I generally work with pieces I already have—ribbon left over from presents or previous Maypoles; pieces of jewelry I no longer wear; any odd or lovely bells, beads, or shells (preferably with holes in them). Choose things already linked to you to add a personal flavor and power to the charm.

A charm is a gentle spell to draw something to you. Your intention for the charm may be love, passion, fertility, or any aspect of these. If you're working with a group, you may choose to all make passion charms, for instance, or you may leave it open for each person to choose what's appropriate in their life at the moment.

You will need:

- Pieces to make the charms with. Each person should bring small items such as bells, shells with holes in them, beads, tiny pieces of fabric, flowers, small feathers, old earrings, or brooches. You can use tokens or charms from other spells or rituals to add power to the charm. You might choose to bind some of your hair into the charm

- Construction aids such as scissors, small pieces of colored card or paper, felt-tip pens, glue, a thin and strong cord for binding, and a few pieces of colored ribbon

- If you want your charms to be contained in a bag or pouch, you will need either small pieces of colored fabric or premade tiny bags

- Essential oil or perfume for anointing your charm (optional)

- Elements for blessing charms with: air, fire, water, and earth (optional)

Time:

- 30 minutes

Intention

Your intention is a major part of a charm, so spend some time clarifying this. You may choose to discuss it or keep it private, but remember the old adage of *be careful what you ask for* and don't leave too many open endings. *I ask for a passionate love* could leave you weeping and bereft for a long time after your passionate love has burned its short course.

Some suggestions for a love charm are: *I ask to be open to deep love, Let me give and receive love in a balanced and full relationship,* or *May I become aware of all that is love.*

Some suggestions for a fertility charm are: *If the universe wishes it, may my desires to become a parent be fulfilled, May I be reminded of my fertile creativity,* or *I remember I am the creatrix of my life.*

Some intentions for a passion charm are: *May I find the path to express my true passions, May my passion bring me joy and fulfillment,* or *I awaken the passion within.*

A Note on Love Spells of All Kinds: It is unethical in the extreme to involve anyone else, by name or intention, in the working of a love spell without their express, current, spoken permission. Think how you would feel if someone you barely knew, didn't like, or found unattractive was aiming a love spell at you. It is generally understood that this type of love spell goes awry and has, at the very least, unpleasant consequences for the caster.

The *only* two acceptable types of love spell are to focus on yourself. The first is in the style of, *I ask that all internal obstacles to me finding a loving relationship be removed.* The second is in the style of, *I ask for love with a person perfect for me.*

Method

I like to make my charms so they can be tied onto something—a May-pole, tree, or wrist—but you could also make charms designed to stick on the wall, sit on your altar, or nestle under your pillow. Decide in advance whether you are making a charm in a bag or a charm to tie onto something.

- Choose a small object to represent yourself (maybe a heart-shaped bead, a symbol you associate with yourself, or something that was yours). Now choose one or more other pieces to represent your intention. You may choose literally (so that if you asked for your passion to get louder you might choose a bell), by association (choosing red or pink things if you asked for love), or just intuitively by feeling out what's appropriate for your own charm.

- Bind the elements of your charm together by stringing them onto a ribbon or cord, making a small plaited bracelet, or place them all into a tiny bag or piece of cloth that can be bound up into a pouch.

- You can write the words of your intention on a small piece of colored card or paper (perhaps in the shape of a heart) and put this in the bag or attach it to your charm.

- If you wish, anoint the charm with a scented oil or bless it with the four elements—air (breath or a feather waved over it), fire (passing it above a candle or holding it in sunlight), water (sprinkling a few drops of water on it, especially water from your altar), and earth (holding it down to the earth, or smearing a little clay or mud on one corner).

- Charge your charm at Beltaine, in your own special ritual, or under the moon with an invocation (maybe to the Goddess of Love or the Horned Lord). Then place the charm where it was intended to go.

Summer Solstice

Celebrated on or close to June 21 in the Northern Hemisphere and December 21 in the Southern Hemisphere.

Summer Solstice

I've been part of many, many Summer Solstice rituals. One year I went to England and ran four or five of them for different groups. In my early thirties, by traveling between hemispheres, I had nine Summer Solstices in a row with no Winter Solstices. It felt wonderful to bounce back and forward between summers; doing so many Summer Solstice rituals was full-on and celebratory and I kept up with the demands of it. I was in a relationship that was like the Summer Solstice—full of blazing love and heat, bold and unstoppable. The Summer Solstice speaks of sacred union; it's the time when the earth is richly giving forth, flowering and fruiting under the sun's attention. This Festival blesses relationships and the recognition of the divine within each one of us. Summer Solstice rituals often involve honoring each other, dancing, singing, and feasting.

It's a very optimistic Festival in both hemispheres. In Australia it falls at the end of the calendar year and gets mixed in with Christmas. It's hot, but usually before drought, bushfires, and dust storms have manifested. It signals holiday time, beaches, and hanging out with friends and family. In Europe, the length of light is often more obvious than actual heat, the real force of summer comes later. But the sheer length of the days signal that darkness and cold are gone for a while and a sense of luxury takes over with enjoying parks, gardens, and visits with friends stretching into the long evenings. It's a sensual time of year, flirting with us, tempting us to express our longings, to indulge, and to be expansive.

Immediately before ending up in New York on 9/11, I'd spent five days in Venice. I was entranced by the Venetian masks—their beauty and ritualized power to conjure an archetype, an echo of another world. I started noticing sun-and-moon motifs with a male sun and a female moon. Each one was a little different, but the sun was always gazing outwards at the viewer while the moon was turned sideways, to face him. One day Damon and I stumbled into a small square with a mask shop, but it was closed. In its window was a magnificent papier-mâché sun-and-moon wall plaque nearly three feet wide and tall, glorious with gold and silver paint. The sun, whose rays rippled like an aura behind and above him, was turned to gaze into the eyes of his companion, the moon, who gazed back at him. They were equals.

Another time we found our way back there by chance (reading a map in Venice is a bit of a joke, and we relied more on the maze-solving capacities we'd honed in actual mazes) and found it shut again. The morning we were to leave Venice was a Sunday, the least likely time for any shop to be open, particularly before 10:00 a.m. I gave us half an hour to find it and, miraculously, we arrived there. The door was open. I went in and bought my sun-and-moon. The man spoke enough English to explain to me the three-day process used to make it, and how he and his brother prided themselves that their work was different from that found elsewhere; they also had a gorgeous north wind, lovely leaf-men, and grain Goddesses.

The sun-and-moon was too large to be packed and too fragile to go under a plane. I carried it with me, swathed in bubble wrap in an enormously oversized yellow plastic bag. I thought we were nearly home. That was before the chaos, endless delays, rerouting and half-a-dozen extra trips imposed by the advent of 9/11. That plaque ended up on buses and subways, spent two days with us in a YMCA camp of displaced passengers, went on four flights to get across the United States, another one to Australia, and a further domestic flight within Australia. Even in the midst of the total disarray of airports, flights, and schedules and in the stringent, suddenly imposed safety crackdowns, each cabin crew found space for it, often in their own jacket locker so it wouldn't be damaged.

I thought if I managed to get it home it would help me find the sacred union I yearned for. Keeping it safe and lugging it through terrorist attacks and their resulting fallout was a test; how much did I want it? This time I sought a man who would gaze not outwards as the blazing God but inward, toward the relationship. When I got it home I hung it on a wall in my house and let it work its magic.

Summer Solstice Memoir

I've been in this relationship for a year and it's extraordinary. I didn't even imagine this—this fierce, deep loving that's incandescent sometimes with pleasure, passion, and a wild freedom. It's as if loving each other is the most radical thing we could do. I've written this ritual to celebrate it; sacred marriage not as some remote, placid thing but as original splendor, burning up in flames and ecstasy. And I want it all—sacred marriage in every dimension. I want union between my lover and myself; I want the union of self within self as well as the union of human with divine. I invite all of them in, into my life and body and into this ritual, the first Summer Solstice ritual I've ever run. This is the day of the longest light, and we've come to honor the powers of the masculine and feminine playing and raging and joining together.

Yesterday I chose two fallen branches for this ritual and sprayed one with gold paint and the other with silver. The leaves lie against each other and glitter in sunlight, trembling, flickering, and whispering when the branch moves; they're eucalyptus, which are surely sacred to this land. The leaves on these trees conserve water by twisting around on the stem to show only an edge to the sun, demonstrating how to exist through our fierce summers. They stand in the hottest sun without burning. The silver branch is like liquid moonlight, so beautiful I can hardly bear to give it away.

We're holding the ritual in the gardens of an old weatherboard house. There are people spilled through the rooms and gathering outside, children, men, and women getting ready. It's a golden day before the fraught unending heat of summer really kicks in. Around the house are orchard-like lawns with trees that are irregularly placed. At the bottom of the garden is a rainforest version of a grove with fig trees and bangalow palms, a bird of paradise plant splashing purple and orange among the rainforest greens. The women are dressed in blue and the men in yellow, orange, and red; we are birds of paradise ourselves and the children wear bright rainbows of every color possible.

I want this ritual to leap into being, to burst out from the energy of the Summer Solstice, and so I've arranged for a man and a woman to be callers, to pick up the gold and silver branches and tear through the house and gardens, shouting for others to join them in the dance of sacred ritual, to come as guests to the marriage of the God and Goddess. I picked one of the women who lives in this house; she was nervous but she also thought the silver branch was beautiful, beautiful enough to risk this running, shouting, leaping part I have devised for her. And for the man I asked my own beloved whose energy shines so bright and sharp I sometimes see him as a warrior of light.

I walk around a corner of the house and see them sitting together on a bench against the wall. They are deep in conversation, leaning toward each other. He has his arm around her shoulders and she has her hand on his leg, on the inside of his leg. I am startled, seeing them like this and stop still. Inexplicable to myself, what I feel is a fierce joy. A small part of me is surprised, even shocked to see him so casually intimate with another woman, one he barely knows, but I gave them these parts, gave them to each other, and I see them struggling to grow into them, to meet before they transform into their separate journeys, sun and moon; he to call the men and she to call the women. It is a moment of such intense privacy that I back away. I feel almost proprietary about their sitting together, as if I am its author and it belongs to me. I walk back into the garden.

Then it begins. I hear her calling out at the top of her voice from within the house and imagine her brandishing her silver branch; he dashes and leaps around the garden with the gold branch with rattling leaves, shouting at the men to join him, to follow, to dance. I go inside and see her running through rooms, calling over her shoulder, and women laugh with her, catch hold of children and each other's hands and come after her while she skips around. The men are more energetic, tearing along in a serpent line around obscure parts of the garden; as the women emerge outside the larger dance begins with the leaders weaving their paths toward one another, and then away. Eventually they start circling each other as two long lines, silver branch and gold branch at the heads, and the double spiral dance begins. We follow as they twist us in, tighter and tighter, a spiral of men and a spiral of women with the kids all mixed up, dashing chaotically between lines and under linked hands in any direction they chose.

The leaders meet each other face to face at the center and lift and clash their branches together, gold and silver leaves gleaming in the sun and shaking with impact, then they turn to wind out. Somehow it works and now the women are snaking down toward the rainforest grove while the men dash and leap in and through the line and away and around again. By the time we get to the mouth of the grove they are arriving side by side, the man and woman with the gold and silver branches and lines of people trailing behind them. The leaves catch and flash in the light, they are out of a fairytale, a myth. By now their faces, when I catch glimpses of them, are altered. His face is grave, intent and focused, lines of concentration and his startlingly blue eyes drawn; hers is flushed and open, laughing and she has forgotten her reservations.

They enter the grove side by side and pause. Then each paces slowly around their side of the grove, meeting again at the altar and leaving behind them an ovoid shape of bodies, men on one side, women and most of the children on the other. They have led our ritual into its beginning, now they place their branches by the altar and become again an ordinary woman—young and awkward, eager and uncertain—and an ordinary man—my beloved, aging, and slightly fierce, taut with concentration.

We cast the circle; the women stand into the center of the grove to call upon the Goddess. We raise our arms as the men tone around us, reaching out with voices and hands for the Goddess energy, welcoming it into our bodies, into the circle, bringing it through. I've asked one woman, anyone, to claim this energy when she feels it strong within her and after a minute a woman steps forward, into the very center. As the calling dies away, I take the silver moon-crown from the altar and place it on her head. Then we call forth the God. Our voices reach out, searching for him, for that full Summer Solstice energy, for the strength of the Horned Lord, the magnificence of the sun king. The Goddess searches the row of men with her eyes, silently asking each one *Is it you? Is it you, today, come to play the God, my lord and partner?* And one of the men meets her eyes and her challenge and steps forward and she offers him the gold sunburst crown she holds in her hands.

Now it is the children's turn, and they leap into their role. Damon, who is only five, is among them, as they decorate the altar with ribbons and lengths of cloth, fern fronds, and special stones and anything else they can find. They are enthusiastic and busy, bower birds bustling and tweaking and arranging, creating a vibrant mess of colors and objects. The altar is the miscellaneous mixed with the sacred, but it is bursting with energy, just like this day of the Summer Solstice. Once they are done, the God and Goddess move among them, blessing each child with the fire of the God and the love of the Goddess.

Seeing these children gravely accepting the blessings, watching the Goddess crouch down to meet them and the God call out his energy to each one of them, I am crying. These are children for whom the God and the Goddess walk the earth, and the plants and rocks and animals are their friends. This is a paradise. In this little exchange between each child and these embodied divinities is a piece of what I wanted for this ritual: the sacred marriage. Each child receives it in their own way; shyly, happily, courteously, overwhelmed, and matter-of-factly.

And then it is our turn. The children cluster around their altar, sitting on parts of it and we ask each man and woman to walk through the grove to where the Goddess and God stand. If they choose, they can walk up with their partner to receive these blessings.

I have never before been in a relationship where I would have expected or accepted to walk together into the realms of sacred marriage. At the very beginning, I was astounded no one had ever told me a relationship could be like this. I had to tell everyone how important I felt it was to say that life contained these possibilities, that something like this existed, was happening, was real. This mutual delight and reverence taught me I could grow and grow and grow in a relationship, not feeling the limits of it. That I could feel loved for my essential being and nothing changed that. That I could find someone who would revel in our joining, in our patterns of merging and difference, someone who would tread the path of spirit so strongly and clearly and seek to walk by my side in it.

The previous Summer Solstice we were still tumbling into that very first knowledge of the depths of the other, and he came into my house, at night, with frangipani blossoms cupped in his hands. In summer they are so plentiful that they lie in the grass under the trees, every day a new carpet of them; their white-and-gold are picked up by children, placed in bowls, or used to decorate an altar. So he brought in this ordinary but still absolutely luxurious flower whose perfume stuns a whole room and he placed them on the bed. He picked one up and spoke of what he saw in me, what beckoned him forward into relationship and he gave me the flower. And then he picked up a second flower and spoke of how he felt, that tremulous, gigantic yearning and excitement, and he gave me that flower also. And I completed the ritual with the other two flowers and I could barely believe it was real.

I stand into the grove when it is my turn and feel how I am ablaze there, fire rising up in me, a challenge and demand and a beckoning all at once; I do not look but I know he will choose to come forward and walk with me. I can feel the clarity of our connection like the next step in a dance, the figures known but each time containing a surprise of the moment—*this* is what it feels like to take his hand, to take these paces forward, to arrive together. The walk down the length of this grove is our sacred marriage and I am the Summer Solstice queen, walking forward into the embrace of her beloved. The Goddess is here, wearing the silver moon crown, the God by her side, for this day they are equal and joined. We bow to them.

The Goddess turns to me; she is all shining gentleness and even though she speaks some words, I have no need of them. For me she is the body of the ritual; hers is the grove, the children, the altar; hers is the singing of the women and the men. The God is blessing my lover, and I see they meet eye to eye and any words spoken are less than that. Then they change places; the Goddess reaches out a hand and touches the face of my beloved and he starts a little, he did not expect to be touched and she whispers her blessing. And meanwhile the God has spoken his ritual words to me, *I bless you with the fire of the God*, and looking at him, looking at them but also at my lover, I want to shout out, to sing, to answer, *I have your blessing and it is him, this man by my side with his golden-bright energy, his willingness, how ferociously he walks through the world. How together the two of us shine more brightly.* I am shining.

I feel them joining inside me, Goddess and God, the sacred union, the Summer Solstice. It's within me; it's walking by my side; it's all around me. We turn and walk back to our places and I have in me not the tiniest piece of wanting left over; it's everything I could ask. I am filled up with this and my loudness and bigness of a moment before is subsumed, like a solar flare returning to its center, and I hold all of this within me; God and Goddess, ritual and relationship, fire and earth. The Summer Solstice.

Sacred Marriage

The Summer Solstice is midsummer, the longest day and shortest night of the whole year. The sun, along with all divine powers associated with it, is at its strongest, and this Festival is dedicated to the glory of light. It is celebrated with the flowers and fruits of summer. This is literally the height of summer; although the weather will continue to warm, once past the Summer Solstice the days get incrementally shorter and the nights lengthen until the Autumn Equinox, three months later, when the nights and days will be equal again. At the Summer Solstice, the sacred marriage between the sun and earth is celebrated.

As the earth changes form throughout the year, so does the Goddess. She is a maiden in spring and becomes lover and fertile mother as the year moves around through Beltaine and the Summer Solstice. She is pregnant (with the year's crops, or next year's God) at Lammas and the Autumn Equinox and metamorphoses into the crone at Samhain (although still carrying her child to be born at Winter Solstice, just as she herself is reborn from crone into maiden). The transitions of the God in this same story are even more dramatic. He is newborn with the sun at Winter Solstice, young and growing throughout the first half of the year, and then already dying or dead at Lammas. At the Autumn Equinox he is present in the fruits of harvest and then he appears as the Lord of the Dead at Samhain. It's at the Summer Solstice he is at his fullest power when he enters into divine union with the Goddess.

Sacred marriage is a challenging concept. By definition its primary meaning is a marriage between Gods. But even they, when we examine their stories, do not inhabit that state continually. The act of sacred marriage is only part of their story, a condition that is realized only briefly, periodically, or seasonally. It's possible to view their entire relationship as a sacred marriage—including his birth and death—but this is not usually what we think of when yearning for sacred marriage to manifest in our own lives. We concentrate on the aspect of union, mutual love, and sexual fulfillment that is only briefly depicted in the cycles of the year. The general understanding of sacred marriage is limited to the lovely idea of two beings joining together, each of them completing the other.

Sacred marriage can be seen as two halves of one whole coming together, reminiscent of a jigsaw puzzle where the parts fit together perfectly. This idea appears in the story Plato tells of the original humans having four arms and four legs until the jealous Gods split them in two, leaving them to search always for their other halves. This story has underpinned the concept of soul mates and also the dialectics of masculine and feminine within our culture, offering the idea that each contains aspects the other does not have, and each needs the other in order to be whole.

Examining this model of sacred marriage we can see it is not dynamic and does not evolve. It leaves little room for growth or change within existing partnerships, and if you don't find your other half, what then? If, on the other hand, you have found your perfect match, imagine the pressure to remain constantly in that perfection! But this story no longer reflects our reality. Serial relationships are now standard, replacing the happily-forever-after monogamy that was until recently the only available model. What were once sharp and defined differences in gender roles are now blurred. Homosexual relationships are widely understood as equally valid expressions of love and partnership. All these factors undermine the classic romantic model of sacred marriage.

A different model of sacred marriage is the union of two wholes rather than two halves; each complete within itself. This leaves room for personal growth as well as change and development within the relationship. Most modern personal development sources recommend this as the best way to create and sustain strong and mature relationship. When these two full beings join together they don't so much provide for each other's missing parts as overlap, bringing two entire beings together. In spiritual practice, also, one may experience oneself as a whole identity in complete, active and entire relationship with the divine; a co-creator, rather than the traditional model of waiting to be filled by the divine force.

Yet another way of understanding sacred marriage is to look at its components (whether these be two humans, two cells, a God and Goddess, or even a multitude of beings) not as discrete identities and not as parts of a whole but as aspects of one thing. The differently colored rays of a rainbow are not objects different from each other. They are aspects of the same object—the rainbow—each viewed differently through the refraction of light. So all Gods or all Goddesses can be understood not as separate from each other, and not all as different pieces of one thing, but as aspects of the same thing perceived in numerous different ways. Following this through at a human level we become not individual pieces of an ultimate oneness, but perceived differences of an absolute oneness.

This would mean that sacred marriage is not two different beings coming together in perfect union, but rather the communion between two perceived differences of the whole which each of them represent. Each is entirely and utterly contained within the other and always has been. Sacred marriage seen in this light symbolizes the universal secret that any *one* is also the entirety of *all*. This concept addresses the conundrum of sacred union between the Gods only occurring during a small part of any year; it renders the sexual union as an aspect of sacred marriage, not its entirety, and says that aspect, as every other aspect, is continually present. It is just, viewed through the lens of the Wheel of the Year, that we are looking at a particular angle at any one time, not that what we are looking at is a different thing from one part of the year to the next.

What does this mean in human terms? I think of sacred marriage as something that occurs between my soul and the divine. And if it were also occurring between my beloved's soul and the divine, then we would have a divine place in which to meet. A place carved out by our individual union with divinity. Our ability to gaze clearly at each other's soul would exist due to our practice in having gazed clearly at our own souls. And in having received, felt, or known something like the clear gaze of divinity through our own souls, we could then draw on this energy to lend our relationship some aspect or understanding of sacred marriage as we relate to each other.

Just as the Summer Solstice represents the fullness of the year—the height of the sun, the burgeoning bounty of the earth—it can represent the fullest point in our own lives. Chronologically we often meet this challenge in our thirties as we move into maturity. Our lives fill up to overflowing with family, relationships, and careers as we strive to succeed on many fronts and experience the realization of our dreams. The Summer Solstice can also represent the high point of any project or undertaking: the publication of a book, launching an art show, the implementation of plans long worked on, or success in a business venture. It may be aligned with joyful and demanding participation in a community or family, or the mature flowering of a relationship.

Across hemispheres the Winter and Summer Solstices occur on the same day. This theme of powerful opposites drawn together or occurring simultaneously (the meeting of two wholes) occurs twice a year on the solstices. The fullness of winter meets the fullness of summer. The two hemispheres are not separate but two halves or aspects of the earth. Thus sacred marriage is occurring worldwide twice a year. As the extremes of winter concur with the extremes of summer, the earth is embraced between them. The Winter and

Summer Solstices together represent the entirety of sacred marriage more fully than any single Festival could do, for it is the union of two equal and opposite powers that represent sacred marriage, whether that be two Gods, two Goddesses, a Goddess and a God, or human beings. It is in their difference from each other that they are proved whole and entire unto themselves. In joining, the deeper truth that they are actually one is revealed.

For all the wild courtship of the lord and lady at Beltaine or Lammas's God dying into the arms of the Goddess, the most potent places of their relationship on the Wheel of the Year are the Winter Solstice when he is born from her and the Summer Solstice where he joins in union with her. Across the hemispheres, we have both parts of this story occurring simultaneously—the two becoming one in sacred marriage and the one becoming two, by giving birth. The union of the two into one in one hemisphere results simultaneously in the separation of one into two by birth in the other hemisphere, and vice versa. It begins to look less like two separate acts, less like one act with two aspects, and more and more like a single act. The sacred marriage of the Goddess and God provides a lens for us to see how we, too, are aspects of the divine, of the Wheel, of the earth, and of each other.

Summer Solstice Ritual

Notes: "Ritual Basics" on page 295 covers many aspects of ritual, including grounding, casting circles, invocations, and participation.

Instructions for the summer mandala exist more fully on page 181.

This ritual is written to include children, but if there are no children present, their sections can be removed from the ritual.

Section 6, "The Men's, Women's, and Children's Groups," is the central part of this ritual.

Ask everyone to bring:
- A handful or two of flower petals

- A package of grain for the summer mandala per person; for example, split peas, pasta, chickpeas, or rice

- A decorative offering for the summer mandala; for example, a special flower, a candle, seedpods, or some beautiful fruits or vegetables locally in season

- Food for the Summer Feast, if you are having one

Other things needed for this ritual:

• A few spare packages of grain (long pasta and brightly colored grains are great)

• Drum/percussion instrument (one or more)

Clothing suggestion:

• Men to wear gold, yellow, red, or orange

• Women to wear earthy greens and browns

• Children to wear bright or rainbow colors

Roles in ritual:

These can all be done by different people or one or two people can take all or most of the roles depending on how confident and experienced the group is:

• Calling directions; this can be done by several different people or all by one person

• Grounding

• Leading warm-ups

• Leading discussion and giving instructions

• Timekeeper (this may not be necessary and can be combined with another role)

• Drummer/song leader

• Facilitators for the men's and women's groups (optional— this is good for a large group)

• Children's group facilitator; if you are planning a separate children's group you may have teenagers who can organize this, or otherwise call for an adult volunteer (often a parent of young children will be happy to take this role)

Length of Ritual: 1.5 hours

Ritual

1. Gathering

Welcome the group to the ritual space and take care of any housekeeping. If some people are unfamiliar with ritual etiquette, briefly explain how you'd like the ritual to run.

Announce the intention of the ritual. For example, *Today we celebrate the Summer Solstice, The intention of this ritual is to acknowledge the longest day of the year*, or *We come together to honor the sacred union of the God and Goddess.*

Ask everyone to introduce themselves briefly. Start with yourself, to give a demonstration of the type of introduction you want. If you have a large group (more than twenty), you can ask people simply to introduce themselves to the person or people next to them.

2. Grounding and Warm-ups

Warm-ups are optional, but great in a group that doesn't know each other well or isn't practiced in ritual, and also in groups with children.

GROUNDING:

- Briefly introduce the idea of grounding; explain that it is done to assist everyone to become more present, feel alive in their bodies, and release distractions.

- Offer a seasonal grounding asking people to begin as a sunflower seed planted in the moist ground. Follow the journey of this seed as it becomes a sunflower, developing petals and seeds and following the sun through the sky. At the end, ask people to themselves fill up with the sun's rays.

- Speak slowly and clearly, adding intonation and variety to your voice as the flower moves through its different stages.

• Finish with a clear instruction for everyone to open their eyes (if they were shut) and become fully present.

SUGGESTED WARM-UPS:

• **Physical:** Full-body expression; ask each person to think of an area of their life they feel full in. In turn, they stand forward and make a statue or a mime representing that area and others guess what it is.

• **Vocal:** Finding your full voice; begin with deep breaths, in and out, and extend into toning, encouraging working with the breath for a full sound. Pair up with someone across the circle and play at stretching the sound (both have to be able to hear each other's tone, but the idea is to stretch it out so there's as much distance between them as possible). Everyone else is doing the same thing simultaneously. Partners should use hand gestures to communicate.

3. Creating a Sacred Space

• **Cast a circle:** Stand in a loose circle, bigger than you want your actual circle to be. Have each person cast their handful or two of flower petals in an arc in front of their feet, so they join up in the shape of a circle. Then ask everyone to step within the circle of petals, acknowledging they are stepping into sacred space.

• **Call to the directions and the elements:** Have four people each calling to one quarter and then together calling Above and Below. You can have two men and two women or pairs for each quarter. Alternatively, it can all be done by one person.

Northern Hemisphere:

East	Air	Rising sun, warmth, growth, and promise
South	Fire	Summer Solstice, the height of the season
West	Water	Long rays of afternoon light, the setting sun
North	Earth	Place of mystery, where the sun's light does not reach

Above and Below

Southern Hemisphere:

East	Air	Rising sun, warmth, growth, and promise
North	Fire	Summer Solstice, the height of the season
West	Water	Long rays of afternoon light, the setting sun
South	Earth	Place of mystery, where the sun's light does not reach

Above and Below

4. Introducing the Summer Solstice

Have one person stand forward and explain the Summer Solstice is the longest day and shortest night of the year. You can mention in the other hemisphere it is the Winter Solstice, the shortest day and longest night.

The Summer Solstice represents fullness, growth, and the power of the sun. It's also when sacred union is celebrated, supported by the strength of the sun and the ripeness of the earth. Summer Solstice is a great time to acknowledge the fullness and blessings in our lives, whether that be in relationships and family, career and creativity, or health and inner well-being.

After the initial explanation, ask each person to contribute their own ideas about what the Summer Solstice or this time of the year means to them, and to the place or land where they live. It may mean a school holiday, a busy time in the garden, or a time of enjoying leisure and family. If it is a large group (over twenty people), you can break into smaller groups for this section.

You might wish to include in the discussion the aspect of the Summer Solstice as fullness, whether that fullness is somewhat stressful or happily received. Bringing the themes of the Summer Solstice closer to home in focusing on relationships and work can be done in a second round of the sharing and will make the ritual more immediate and relevant.

5. Learning the Chant

Introduce the chant or chants you will be using later in the ritual. There are many chants on CDs, online, and in songbooks. You may already have favorite chants that are well-known to your group. You might also have a songwriter among you. Choose a simple song or chant that is true to the themes of your ritual and teach it to the group by singing it a couple of times and then teaching it line by line. It's useful to sing it through together at least eight or ten times, so when you begin singing later in the ritual everyone can easily join in without being having to be reminded of the words or tune.

6. Men's, Women's, and Children's Groups

Depending on how many and the ages of children attending the ritual, you can either have a children's group or not. If there are teenagers present, they are often happy to take charge of this group. Otherwise, children can remain with a parent in the men's or women's group. The groups will have about twenty minutes to half an hour together, and their enactments should be between two and five minutes long.

The men's group should:

• Discuss what the concept of sacred union or sacred marriage means to each

• Talk about where they are personally, with relationships in their life, self-love, and love of and union with the divine

• Discuss and then create an honoring of the women as part of the ritual. They may choose to honor the women as their friends, lovers, and family; as the Goddess; or as their spiritual sisters. This honoring can take the form of dance, song, a movement-based piece, or anything else

The women's group should:

• Discuss what the concept of sacred union or sacred marriage means to each

• Talk about where they are personally, with relationships in their life, self-love, and love of and union with the divine

- Discuss and then create an honoring of the men as part of the ritual. They may choose to honor the men as their friends, lovers, and family; as the God; or as their spiritual brothers. This honoring can take the form of dance, song, a movement-based piece, or anything else

The children's group should:
- Create a blessing for the men's and women's groups (together or separately)

Each group then presents their offering to the whole group.

7. Summer Mandala

This activity is fully described on page 181, immediately after the ritual.

Explain a mandala is a geometric pattern used for contemplation and focus. It is often circular and usually divided into equal segments. If you have a specific intention for the summer mandala, such as happiness, love, or healing for the world, announce that.

Each person in turn uses their package of grain to help create the mandala. One person may begin with a circle of split peas, the next add some spokes of pasta, the next add small piles of kidney beans in the center of each segment, and so on.

Once all the grains are used up, take a moment to admire the mandala.

Then ask each person to bring their special offering and place it into the mandala. They can speak if they choose. Someone may wish that love will spread out to those who need it; another may wish that their health will return fully, another that they will find a relationship where they feel fulfilled.

8. Raising Energy

If you have a drummer or percussionist, they can lead into the chant by beginning with the beat. Start gently, reminding others of the words and tune, and gradually increase the energy of the song. You might like to dance around the mandala, becoming wilder as the energy rises and developing a cone of power, bringing the chant to its height and waiting until everyone is fully extended with their voice and energy and movement before releasing it in a single, high-pitched tone or a shout.

9. Complete the Ritual

Acknowledge the directions and elements in the reverse order that they were called and dissolve the circle. Generally, the same people who called them do this.

- **Acknowledge the directions and elements:**

Northern Hemisphere:
Below and Above

North	Earth	Place of mystery, where the sun's light does not reach
West	Water	Long rays of afternoon light, the setting sun
South	Fire	Summer Solstice, the height of the season
East	Air	Rising sun, warmth, growth, and promise

Southern Hemisphere:
Below and Above

South	Earth	Place of mystery, where the sun's light does not reach
West	Water	Long rays of afternoon light, the setting sun
North	Fire	Summer Solstice, the height of the season
East	Air	Rising sun, warmth, growth, and promise

- **Release the circle:** This circle was cast by everyone with flower petals, so ask each person to acknowledge they are leaving sacred space as they step back over the boundary (which may have vanished or been scattered by now anyway) and back into ordinary space.

Thank each person for coming and for the energy they have contributed and begin the Summer Feast if you are having one.

I like to leave my mandalas where they've been made—removing anything not biodegradable or edible, such as candles. The mandalas look quite lovely over the following days, as animals, birds, and weather gradually break them down.

Summer Solstice
Activity: Summer Mandala

You can make a mandala by yourself, with your family, or with a group of others. It can be done as part of a ritual or simply as an offering to the earth. Even very small children love to do this—it's a winning combination of using food for unorthodox purposes and leaving the offering in the garden for the birds and fairies. If you don't have a garden, use a wildish (or neglected) section of a public park. Making a mandala by yourself can be very meditative, while making it with a group—either as a stand-alone ritual or part of a larger ritual—is generally joyous and celebratory.

You will need:
- A variety of materials for the mandala. You can use grains, dried legumes, and pasta as the main components. The mandala can also be made using fruit and vegetables, leaves, flowers, sticks, and pinecones if you are in a forest, or if you are on the beach, collect shells, feathers, and seaweed or whatever is to hand. Make sure all

your components are natural and biodegradable. If this is done in a group, ask each person to bring some of these items. If you are doing it at home with small children, raid the pantry for any out-of-date, left-over or unused items; the more exotic the better

- You may also wish to bring decorative items such as candles, statues, and bowls of water that you place into the finished mandala and then remove when you leave. Never leave any burning candles unattended, and depending where you live there may be a total fire ban during summer, making any naked flame outside not only dangerous but also illegal

- A camera to record your finished mandala (optional)

Time:
- 30 minutes

Intention

If you are working with a group, having an intention for the mandala assists in maintaining focus. Each person can also make individual contributions toward the intent. For example, if the intent is, *To honor the earth*, each person can then make their offering (as they contribute to the mandala) to fit into the larger intent. For example, *I will honor my own garden this summer, I will work for the clean water campaign, I will teach my children where food comes from*, or *I will lobby the Council about planting native trees*. Other examples of intents are, *To offer and receive love and joy* or *To deepen our awareness of the sacred nature of all life*. An intention can be set by you or decided on by the group before the mandala-making commences.

Method

This is an outdoor ritual; not that it is impossible to make the mandala indoors, but part of the point is leaving it outside as an offering (particularly if it is made of food items) for the birds and the earth.

• If you are making the mandala with other people but not as part of a larger ritual, it's great to introduce the theme of the Summer Solstice by talking about the day and what it represents. You could include a discussion about the longest day (regarding the relative positions of the sun and earth); what it means to you personally, and what summer means to others, as well as some of the deeper themes of the Summer Solstice.

• Make your concept of the mandala clear if you are with a group or with children. Explain how large it is going to be, the basic shape (usually a circle), and how the segments will be filled in. If you want it to be mainly symmetrical, say so. Explain how various items can be used. You can make spokes or separating lines inside the mandala (defining the edges and segments). You can make patterns inside the sections of the mandala (for example, a pile of corn kernels in the middle of each segment). You can outline or fill in other shapes. The materials each person has brought will help decide this; spaghetti is great for defining segments of the mandala, rice or chickpeas may work well for a border, flowers or red lentils may be perfect for the center or clumped within sections.

• Discuss or set the intention for the mandala. If you expect each person to also speak an intent or offering as they contribute to the mandala, give clear examples of this. You may prefer to work in silence or with a chant. If you are making the mandala solo, enter a meditative mindset after setting your intention, or chant aloud or under your breath.

• Begin with the outline of the mandala and continue creating it with people taking turns to contribute. With children, there can be a lot of discussion, consultation, and help in pouring the different grains and colors, or placing things how they want them. It's an organic process and no two mandalas ever look alike. Mandalas using found items (for example, at a beach or in a park, where everyone is given ten minutes to collect whatever they can find and bring it back) vary even more widely.

• If you have brought decorative items such as candles or statuettes, add them to the finished mandala.

• It's lovely to take photos of your summer mandala. You can share them with others or collect them over the years to show off all the different ones.

• Spend some time enjoying your mandala, chanting or meditating beside it or feasting around it.

Lammas

*Celebrated on August 2 in the Northern Hemisphere
and February 2 in the Southern Hemisphere.*

Lammas

The very first Wheel of the Year ritual I held was a Lammas ritual. About forty people came; the men drew lots to see who would take the part of the Grain God. The lot fell upon Damon's father, who shouted out with fierce joy. Damon was five and he huddled close to my best friend, whispering to her that he didn't have parents anymore because his mother was the priestess and his father was the God. Later in the ritual, Damon watched his dad carried in by the men, their arms outstretched to hold his dad high in the air; Damon heard the women grieving the death of the God, down on the ground. The moment when a child realizes his parents are more than just his parents, or when the wider picture is abruptly and shockingly revealed, is deeply relevant to Lammas.

One year I watched all the men, not just one, die in their enactment. They selected one man to be the reaper. As the men danced, the reaper came to them, one by one, and felled them. I watched my lover die in this way and though I had always seen him as a man accepting of death, who would go to it willingly, he struggled in this enactment, fought back as the reaper grappled to lay him down and that struggle distressed me deeply. Damon was at my side. Years later, Damon was at my side again; in a ritual where half of us were chosen by lot to die, he sat silently by my "dead" body—he was so silent I did not even know he was there.

I had worried about the rawness of this, and what might be considered an unnecessary level of exposure for a child to the concept of death, even though a child in another culture, time, or place might see far more, unguarded. My concern was that these sometimes violent and powerfully enacted deaths at Lammas were provocative; compared with Samhain when we lit a candle for each person who'd died in the previous year. Samhain was a quiet, heartfelt acknowledgement that brought real death home in an unavoidable and reverent way.

The Lammas Festival when Damon was sixteen, he was chosen to play the God because his birthday fell closest to the ritual date. Then the Goddess was chosen by lot, a short stick and it fell to me. Although I had occasionally played the Goddess, and Damon had often played the God, that combination had never happened before. While the others prepared their enactments, Damon spoke to me about Lammas. Each thing he said I was astounded by, in awe of. This was a trained ritual magician, a young man holding and channeling the God energy. The enactment we decided on was simple. I would give birth to him. He would grow and we would dance together. He would die in my arms. All the world would mourn. He said the death should be in war, as wars of invasion were a strong current topic. Even though the thought of him on a battlefield—at all, let alone dying there—was excruciating, I agreed.

When he emerged from under my dress, of course I remembered giving birth to him. When we danced, I looked at him, taller than me, and marveled. And then we crouched on a battlefield, dodging bullets and running forward in short bursts. Damon was shot and called out briefly and fell on his side to the floor and I rushed to him and cried a terrible cry and I was Morrigan on the battlefields and I was Isis bereft and I was Mary beneath the cross and I was also Damon's mother, splitting into ferocious gratitude for him and tearing grief at the fragility of his life.

And I knew from his understanding, and his willingness and grace in acting out this part, that it was justified to have exposed him over the years to the edges of Lammas. He held it within him, perhaps more surely and certainly than I ever would. He did not rail against this Festival, the one of them all I have found the most difficult to accept with its themes of beauty ending prematurely, the beginning of the great stripping away that will eventually culminate in rebirth at the Winter Solstice. He knew the Wheel from the inside and he gave himself to its turning.

Lammas Memoir

This ritual was created by Cathryn, Trinda, and Jane.
In Australia we celebrate Lammas in early February, after our December Summer Solstice. On Boxing Day, December 26, 2004, an earthquake occurred in the Indian Ocean resulting in a tsunami, which killed over 230,000 people in Indonesia, Sri Lanka, India, Thailand, and ten other countries. Photographs in the Australian papers included bays of floating wreckage, among which could be seen dead bodies and parts of bodies. Less than a month later we were still reeling from the event, as the shocking images and stories continued to emerge. It was one of the biggest natural disasters in recorded history.

It happened to be three women who gathered to plan our Lammas ritual. We talked about the tsunami, and how Lammas has always included elements of sudden death, sacrifice of the young and strong, mourning, and loss. We linked that time of year with the nearby extinct volcano, because it was northwest of us, the direction of Lammas when you lay the Wheel of the Year over a compass in the Southern Hemisphere. That volcano's explosion more than twenty million years ago carved out the caldera in which we live. So our whole region—our fertile soil, the rainforest, the cliffs rimmed around us—carries the imprint of that ancient eruption. What today would be a massive natural disaster actually created our beautiful valleys we live in so happily.

We felt the ritual had to have the immensity of elemental powers and the fragility of human life as major themes. We talked about death and disaster. Even though Southeast Asia was so close to us geographically it still seemed Australians were distanced from the tragedy by issues of race, wealth, and culture; while watching and listening to the news we were able to say, *That couldn't be us.* Whereas the Lammas theme brings death home, as close to home as can be. *This sheaf of grain is my son, my lover.* And the very notion of natural disaster is that it can only be escaped by luck and happenstance.

We decided we wanted the ritual to ask how it would be if our seemingly safe little valley was suddenly inundated with water, fire, or plague. What if suddenly and dramatically half our neighbors, friends, and family were dead? The more we spoke the stronger and more necessary this theme became, and the more powerfully it resonated with Lammas. We were a little frightened at the magnitude of what we were creating, so we decided not just to invoke the Goddess at the beginning of the ritual, but also, as there were three of us, we would hold the triple aspects of the Goddess ourselves containing the entire ritual. I was assigned the mother aspect.

On the day of the ritual the three of us wore white. We cast the circle into eight directions and Above and Below, making a strong container. Each person calling spoke of that direction's place in the growing cycle, of seeds and new life, birth, youth, flowering, maturity, of fruits and grains, old age, death, and rebirth. The three of us stood in the center of the circle and called in the Goddess. *Great mother! Goddess of Earth, of this sacred land we live on and walk on, that our bodies are made of and return to! Hold us within your arms. Let us feel your arms around us, in life and also in death. Encompass us within your great circle of living and dying! We honor you and we call to you, Earth Goddess!*

Then we talked of our geography, the fertile caldera, and we built an altar in the northwest. Everyone had brought a symbol of an incomplete project to the ritual—a school assignment, a house being built, a half-written book, a relationship being nurtured—and we placed these symbols on the altar, speaking of our projects and what we hoped and planned. Incomplete projects reflect the incompleteness of Lammas when it is not known if the harvest will be successful and our concealed theme of sudden, unexpected death.

We introduced the idea of elemental powers. Lammas falls between the Summer Solstice, associated with fire, and the Autumn Equinox, associated with water. Fire and water echo the Pagan "calling for the rains" ritual that is held in parts of Australia at this time to break the heat and dry of summer. Fire and water are also reminiscent of the ages-old fire of the volcano and the way clouds always cling to its peak. We talked about the intensity of this season in Australia—the heat, bushfires, and drought, as well as the Lammas theme of the fallen or sacrificed king.

We divided into a fire group and a water group and began discussing our relationships to those elements to create a ritual piece exploring the element's raw force. About fifteen minutes passed in an industrious hum before Cathryn quietly excused herself from her group to begin the interrupter ritual, or ritual-within-the-ritual. I love these interrupter rituals. When they are done carefully (and rarely and delicately) they tip the entire ritual deeply into the realm of the sacred where we are no longer just enacting a ritual but have become living ritual.

In the kitchen, Cathryn screamed at the top of her voice and started bashing a frying pan and lid together, fast and jaggedly. She rushed back into the ritual space, her hair wild and her face overwrought with emotion (probably a mixture of terror and excitement at her own behavior). She screamed at us to, *Get up, move fast, quick this is an emergency, there's no time.* People reacted slowly with amazement and uncertainty. Later someone told me they thought Cathryn had gone mad. She held a handful of wooden popsicle sticks and waved them at us in between beating on her makeshift drum.

Take one, she screamed, *You have to take one of these! Everyone take one!* and bemused, people began gradually taking sticks from her. She lowered her arm so the children could reach. In the kitchen she had counted them so there were exactly the right number, one for every person there. Half of them had blue writing on them, which said, *You are still alive.* The other half had red writing, which said, *You are dead. Lie down now.* Cathryn was a plague bearer, or the wave of the tsunami itself, the Goddess of Death. In our Triple Goddess we cast, Cathryn held the crone. The final stick, whichever it was, would be hers.

The ritual changed completely. Some people took sticks, and some fell to the floor around Cathryn. Others moved away, reading their blue stick in a puzzled way, trying to make sense of it. Others still clung to their elemental group, attempting to coordinate ideas of how to get their enactment working. Cathryn kept shouting, thrusting her hand with the sticks toward people.

I knew what was happening; I had planned this ritual. Still, it was alarming, still my heart beat faster, and I felt things were moving far too rapidly. Damon had been in the water group with me and we moved together toward Cathryn. He was just twelve and happened to be standing in front of me as we both reached up our hands for a stick; it felt momentarily as if he were in the circle of my arms and I thought at least if we die, it will be together. But I caught a glimpse of my stick as I pulled it from Cathryn's hand and it had red writing on it.

I wrote the program myself, it was so strong in me that I started falling to the floor, but in that second, I lost track of my son. It's as if he was wrenched away from me. My eyes closed, but as they closed I hadn't seen him. Where had he gone? Had he fallen down too, and was now lying to one side of me? Was he still standing? How could I not have been watching him? How could I not even know if he was alive or dead?

I lay on the floor, in my dead role as the ritual progressed. I heard the quiet murmur of voices after the tumult; we had bargained, when we planned the ritual, that surely one of us would still be alive and I could hear Trinda's voice, who'd held the maiden. She spoke to the survivors and then I heard her moving among the dead. She came to me and held my hand and whispered something, a blessing, but all I wanted to know was if my son was alive or dead, and she did not tell me that. I listened, straining among hushed voices for the sound of his and I did not hear it. Dead, then? But not within my arms? Dead and alone, I let go of him at the crucial moment. I waited to hear someone crouch behind me, where I thought he must lie, to arrange him or bless him or sing to him, but I couldn't pick it out.

We had agreed this part of the ritual would last ten minutes with no instructions, unless we absolutely had to pull people back on track. It was a long time I lay there, and I felt none of the peace or gentleness I've experienced in other death-oriented rituals. All I had was panic and distress and fierce regret; why wasn't I holding him, how could I not know, how could I have turned away at that exact instant, why hadn't I stayed alive a second or two longer, at least to know if he was dead or would live? Where is he? Why can't I hear him, feel him; and if he's alive, why doesn't he come and tell me? Why doesn't anyone tell me?

I know now that one man sat by his dead son the entire ten minutes and said prayers for his soul. He said later it was a great privilege. I know now that Cathryn was left with a blue stick, which meant she lived though she had brought death to half of us. I know now my son watched me die, and his father die, and also the man I was living with, his stepfather, die. His best friend died. He literally had no one left; though there were adults still alive who could have cared for him, somehow no one did. Later they told me he seemed self-contained. I know now he sat completely silent by my body, waiting.

Finally the chimes were rung to indicate that part of the ritual was over. No amount of relief at leaving behind that desperate headspace of mine could wipe out the impact of the ritual. I am the woman in the flood whose baby is snatched out of her arms. I am the woman away from the village for the day whose house and family are vanished when she returns. I am the woman running along the beach hoping to save my child, but I don't get there in time and I am lifted away from her. I am the woman searching in the ruins. Mine is the child with no parent, no family left. Mine is the child who watched his parents die.

Our plan was to sing, but we were almost speechless, almost wordless. Eventually a chant came together, and at the end of it someone wanted to know when we were doing our elemental enactments; he was disbelieving to learn we were not. Instead we gathered on the floor and made a Lammas Dolly somberly; each person contributing some grain-on-the-stalk, and feeling sharply the edge of life and death that the grain represents. We offered it into the northwest, to the mountain, placing it on our altar.

We made sure to debrief with every person as well as dissolving the circle and grounding. Even though I listened to many other experiences of that ritual, it is my own experience that cemented in my brain; an overriding panic and wild grief I did not anticipate. That I could not die quietly, I could not accept death not knowing what had happened to my child. I could have survived if he died; it was the not knowing that meant I could not let go. My own experience was unusual; on the whole, those who died in the ritual had an easier time of it, most explaining it was quite peaceful. Some of the survivors were at least momentarily harrowed.

It was one of the great rituals we've done. Partly because the mechanics of it worked superbly to explore our themes of sudden death, incomplete projects, the powers of the elements and the fragility of human lives. Partly because every person there entered deeply into the ritual realm, giving our play of death a seriousness and genuineness that brought us toward closing the gap between our privileged selves and those who live in far less privileged places, where this kind of death rate is common in a disaster. And partly because I remember it vividly, over eight years later, as one of the strongest and most unsettling experiences of death I have had. I was carrying the mother aspect of the Goddess, of course. And what is it like for the mother, when her child is ripped away from her? And is not each stalk of grain a child of her womb? Surely, that understanding goes straight to the heart of Lammas.

The Stripping Away

Traditionally, Lammas celebrates the first part of the harvest. It brings to mind dances in barley fields, long summer afternoons, and the promise that hard work will result in a storehouse of grain for the winter. For many years, I was nearly always in England at Lammas, missing the Australian Imbolc, but then I was home again in time for (another) Lammas. I've been at more Lammas rituals than any other Festival. The season is a confusion of golden grain in the English fields and the transition from the hot to the wet season in the Australian rainforest. I hold in my mind ideas of Gods dying in the fields overlapping with people calling on the rains to arrive. Damon is a central part of my memories of Lammas; he was with me on both sides of the world, baking bread and watching Gods die.

The idea of sacrifice, a young man meeting his death in the fields, or even stories of John Barleycorn being mown down by the reapers, showcases the more sinister side of Lammas. Like so many of these Festivals, Lammas seems to contain contradictory themes, in this case promise and loss. Even though the world most of us live in has moved away from such agrarian calendars, from dancing in fields and from harvests being contained to any single part of the year, the Lammas symbolism is still strong. The very notion of sacrifice at a time of hope or of youth meeting with death is a contradiction we find nearly intolerable. Perhaps part of the power this Festival retains comes down to that paradox.

To look at Lammas in a modern context, this loss of life—particularly youthful life—is strikingly relevant when we consider the wars we continue to engage in year after year and generation after generation, sending our young men and women off to foreign lands to kill and be killed. We sacrifice them in the hope that our harvest (our economy and ideology in the form of political and religious institutions) will benefit. In the so-called First World we are in the privileged position of not being invaded ourselves, but we can easily imagine—as the media brings to our attention—the horrors of civilians, including children, who die as a kind of detritus in these wars. There is also the continuing spectrum of natural disasters that come with images of sudden loss and devastation; these are now more immediate than ever, as every story can be viewed in our living rooms or even on our phones within a day of its happening. We see families, villages, and livelihoods ripped apart—destroyed by volcanoes, earthquakes, tidal waves, and famines.

When we align the Wheel of the Year with our life cycle, Lammas comes just after midlife, around the years of our late forties. That's the time when cancer, heart attacks, and other events of mortality strike suddenly into the community of our peers who have been in the very thick of life with growing families, careers, house payments, and community involvements at full force. That's the time of a midlife crisis, when someone apparently successful comes to a place of deep and unsettled questioning about the meaning or value of their life. Classically it's a time for divorces, for men to find younger wives or women to break out into a new life for themselves once their children are grown. For women, particularly, it can also be a crisis of fertility and attractiveness as they face menopause and the limits of their childbearing years, whether or not they have had the children they wished for. Along with this comes a sinister message of fading desirability; the belief that younger women are intrinsically more attractive is probably never so threatening as when we are just passing out of this fertile phase ourselves.

Lammas is the first part of the harvest in the growth-and-decay cycle of the Wheel of the Year. Thus, during Lammas it is relevant to ask ourselves what we are on track to achieve, what has meaning to us, and what exactly we are planning to harvest in this privileged, wealthy world of ours. We may keep our eyes on immediate goals such as completing a project or consolidating our meditation practice or fitness regime; on longer-term goals such as raising children to independence, paying off a house, or securing a promotion; or we may look at the whole of our lives. Does this symbolic first part of our harvest—particularly if we are in midlife—represent something we are proud to own? Or is it completely off-track, lacking meaning, substance, or joy? If so, we may have to deeply question our direction and our choices. Some also choose to examine their lives of relative plenty and decide it is time to make sacrifices; for example, taking in foster children, volunteering time to a charity or cause, or even uprooting and offering skills and energy to a community in poverty, war, or strife.

Looking at the position of Lammas on the Wheel of the Year, I see something very interesting. From the seed point of the Winter Solstice and all the way through to the height of the Summer Solstice, it's all growth; onward, upward, and outward. One minute past the Summer Solstice, though—or one minute into Lammas—and there's a change. The Wheel has turned, and not just the incremental turning it does continually. This is a turn that to human eyes looks more dramatic. We were on the increase—now we're on the decrease. We were focused on the outer—now the focus has switched to the inner. Everything was getting bigger, better, and more—suddenly it's getting less, smaller, and slower.

This is the matrix of Lammas. The year is wrenched around and suddenly nothing is as it was, everything is seen in a different light. Though this provides for new insights, we often experience these as painful. That first

Lammas ritual where my son saw his parents as lost to him is an example of this. Although his parents were still there and still the same people we had always been, suddenly he saw us as separate from him. He understood what had always been the case, that we existed outside of and apart from our roles as his parents. He saw things through the eyes of Lammas. Lammas reveals the essence of things. It teaches us that this beautiful golden grain is actually going to be cut down, that our life requires a death (even if only death of the grain, but also that each life carries its own death within it), and that my father or mother has a life beyond me. Lammas is the beginning of the great stripping away that culminates in the Winter Solstice.

Lammas is the time when the beginning of autumn can be felt even though the days may still be long. We mourn and celebrate the death of the king, of the grain, of the summer lord, who even though he reigned at the height of his powers only moments earlier at the Summer Solstice is already shifting, turning on his downward movement into the earth and the renewing womb of the Goddess.

This is one of the tipping points of the Wheel of the Year. A tipping point is where just a small amount of weight added to one side will cause the whole scale or system to overbalance. Imbolc is in a similar position, just past the other solstice, but because at Imbolc we are tipping into sunlight, growth, and increase, we're not so fussed by it. We welcome it calmly, as if it were our due. But try to take anything away from us, like at Lammas, and we're up in arms. We live in a world where it is expected that not just the share markets and size of the crops and our bank balance will continue to increase, but also other quite intangible things will continue to increase, such as our sense of personal worth, our happiness, and our satisfaction with life. Whether these things increase steadily or exponentially, we don't mind as long as it's on the increase. No decrease. Not loss, death, slowing down, or going backward, not having things culled or stripped back.

At Lammas everything that has culminated in the peak of the Summer Solstice changes; it is surrendered, harvested, transformed. It may be the traditional grain cut down or it may be the fiery hot season giving way to the ferocious, flooding wet. It may be that just as we reach a peak in career, in material accumulation, in wealth, or acclaim we tire of the relentless upward journey and begin to desire something else. It may even be that we look at our achievements and find them hollow. It correlates with part of the aging process, that our bodies begin to change—not temporarily—lessening in their vigor, tautness, and easy good health. We lose a tooth, our skin stretches, we find lines and gray hair and our vision or hearing begins to waver. It's the stripping away, and although incremental it has only one direction—toward death. At Lammas we grapple not just with the sudden death of youth or glory, but also with the inevitable old age and death plodding toward us.

And yet in stories, particularly in fairy tales or myths, what I identify as the Lammas point is the exact point where the story begins to get interesting. In a classic fairytale, there is a beautiful princess or three brothers. The outline of the story is described—they grew up, they had such-and-such personalities, they looked like this or like that. Perhaps a hardship or two exists along the way; there was a stepmother, or the kingdom was too small for three, but nothing untoward happens. Until *bang*. The princess grows into a woman, or the eldest son reaches twenty-one, or the happy kingdom is laid siege to by a dragon, monster, or evil wizard. The whole story must now change into a story of adventure, challenge, daring, and luck. The fairy tale, in effect, has begun.

Are we interested in stories where everything is wonderful and the main character is successful and happy and all continues? Not really. Give us stories of disaster, miscalculation, a sudden turn in fortunes, the tipping of the Wheel. I believe our interest in this moment of change is much deeper than any ghoulish satisfaction we may gain from seeing a successful (perhaps even arrogant or unheeding) character meet their comeuppance. I think our fascination engages at this tipping point because this is when the story gains complexity. Now one's character will be tested, now the deeper truths will begin to be seen. As we strip away the bright dross of achievements and attributes we have been gifted or born with, we began to see where intent, will, a pure heart, true magic, or a burning vision will take us.

This is the call of Lammas. Will we be brave enough to strip away the structures, habits, and activities we are used to in order to find what has meaning for us? Will we begin that work not in mourning for what will be lost, but in celebration? Do we dare to age boldly, not trying to cling to the accouterments of youth but instead boring down into the core of ourselves and culling where necessary to discover our true worth? Like the prince in the fairytale, will we leave our rich heritage behind us to journey out into the world where we are needed? Like the princess, will we abandon luxury and ease, risking everything to follow the path of mystery? If we are agile enough to step to one side as the scythe sweeps through our lives, changing the landscape with the harvest, then we move forward on adventure. And this adventure is marked by the second half of the Wheel, the inward turn. At Lammas we are beckoned within.

Lammas Ritual

Notes: "Ritual Basics" on page 295 covers many aspects of ritual, including grounding, casting circles, invocations, and participation.

Instructions for making the Lammas Dolly exist more fully on page 215.

This ritual is written to include children, but if there are no children present, their sections can be removed from the ritual.

Section 6, "The God, Goddess, and Children's Groups" is the central part of this ritual.

Ask everyone to bring:

- Some grain-on-the-stalk (this can be grass, reeds, wheat or barley, stalks of corn with corn cobs attached, sunflowers, or other flowers or plants that have gone to seed)

- An offering representing the first part of their harvest

- Food for the Lammas Feast, if you are having one

Other things needed for this ritual:

- String or ribbon

- Strong scissors/pruning sheers

- An altar; this can be simple or complex

- A freshly baked loaf of bread

- Drum/percussion instrument (one or more)

Clothing suggestion:

- Adults wear harvest colors (brown, gold, or yellow), children wear bright colors

Roles in ritual:

These can be all done by different people or one or two people can take all or most of the roles depending on how confident and experienced the group is:

- Casting the circle and calling directions (done by several different people or one person)

- Invocations (done by three people; these can be the same as those who called the directions)

- Grounding

- Leading warm-ups

- Leading discussion and giving instructions

- Timekeeper (this may not be necessary, or can be combined with another role)

- Drummer/song leader

- Facilitators of God group, Goddess group, and children's group (optional)

Length of Ritual: 1.5 hours

Ritual

1. Gathering

Welcome the group to the ritual space and take care of any housekeeping. If some people are unfamiliar with ritual etiquette, briefly explain how you'd like the ritual to run.

Announce the intention of the ritual. For example, *Today we celebrate Lammas, traditionally the beginning of the harvest, The intention of this ritual is to acknowledge our place in the Wheel of the Year,* or *We come together to honor the Harvest God and the Earth Goddess.*

Ask everyone to introduce themselves briefly. Start with yourself, to give a demonstration of the type of introduction you want. If you have a large group (more than twenty), you can ask people simply to introduce themselves to the person or people next to them.

2. Grounding and Warm-ups

Warm-ups are optional, but are great in a group that doesn't know each other well or isn't practiced in ritual as well as in groups with children.

GROUNDING:

- Briefly introduce the idea of grounding; that it is done to assist everyone to become more present, feel alive in their bodies and let go of any distractions.

- Offer a seasonal grounding following the journey of a seed. Begin with the seed lying in the dark ground, then cracking open, next sending out roots and its first sprout, growing up into the world, and finally being harvested, or falling to the ground to begin the cycle again.

- Speak slowly and clearly, adding intonation and variety to your voice as the seed moves through its different stages.

- Finish with a clear instruction for everyone to open their eyes (if they were shut) and become fully present.

SUGGESTED WARM-UPS:

- **Physical:** Movement groups; ask the group to become a field of corn; then half the group becomes the wind blowing through the corn and the corn responds. The wind group becomes the sun ripening the corn with the corn responding again. Then they become rain, feeding the corn. Finally, they harvest the corn.

- **Vocal:** Growing voices; have everyone make the sounds they feel a seed might make within itself; next, have everyone make the sounds of rain on the earth; then, have everyone make the sound of the seed cracking open. Try toning together the sound of roots growing down, then of the sprouting, then of leaves unfurling. This can become an impromptu, wordless song.

3. Creating a Sacred Space

- **Cast a circle:** If you want to give your circle casting a particularly Lammas flavor, this can be done with a line of flour sprinkled onto the floor or ground. Otherwise have someone walk around the perimeter of your circle using their hand or a magical tool to draw the outline of the circle.

- **Call to the directions and the elements:** Have four people each call to one direction and then all call Above and Below. This can also all be done by one person. For Lammas, a Cross-Quarter Festival, call to the Cross-Quarters.

Northern Hemisphere:

Northeast	Earth and air	First sprouts of new growth
Southeast	Air and fire	Saplings, buds, grain growing
Southwest	Fire and water	Ripening, fruit forming, harvest
Northwest	Water and earth	Seeds saved, storehouses, fallow fields

Above and Below

Southern Hemisphere:

Southeast	Earth and air	First sprouts of new growth
Northeast	Air and fire	Saplings, buds, grain growing
Northwest	Fire and water	Ripening, fruit forming, harvest
Southwest	Water and earth	Seeds saved, storehouses, fallow fields

Above and Below

- **Invocations:** One person invokes the Earth Goddess, another invokes the Grain God, and a child invokes the power of seeds.

4. Introducing Lammas and Offerings

Have one person stand forward and explain a little about Lammas. Include the information that it is the festival of grain, and the first part of the harvest. At Lammas the twin themes of fertility and death are present. The Grain God dies—is reaped—while the Goddess is pregnant with new life—like a storehouse filled with food. You might also like to include local information relevant to where you are; for example, in my part of Australia, Lammas is clearly the time of the hot season giving way to the wet season or the sun king being overturned by the rains.

Ask each person to contribute their own ideas about Lammas or what this time of year means to them. It may mean hard work, the beginning of the school year, or a time of oppressive heat. It may be a literal harvest for some, as they gather food from their farm or vegetable garden, while for others it may have personal relevance of an anniversary, birthday, or other significant yearly events. If it is a large group (over twenty people), you can break into smaller groups for this section.

You may wish to include in the discussion the aspect of Lammas as a contradictory time of celebrating while also acknowledging inevitable ends. This can be relevant to a particular stage of life (for example, middle age, the raising of young children, or a pregnancy near term) or a project coming to fulfillment. Bringing the themes of Lammas closer to home than abstract discussions of harvest and wheat fields (particularly if you are not in a rural area) can be done in a second round of the sharing and will make the ritual much more immediate and relevant.

Finally, ask each person to come forward and place their offering on the altar, representing the first part of their harvest. Ask them to explain what it is and what it means to them. It's good to go first so you give a clear demonstration of what you are asking for.

5. Learning the Chant

Introduce the chant or chants you will be using later in the ritual. There are many chants on CDs, online, and in songbooks. You may already have favorite chants that are well-known to your group. You might also have a songwriter among you. Choose a simple song or chant that is true to the themes of your ritual and teach it to the group by singing it a couple of times and then teaching it line by line. It's useful to sing it through together at least eight or ten times, so when you begin singing later in the ritual everyone can easily join in without being having to be reminded of the words or tune.

6. God, Goddess, and Children's Groups

Divide into a God group, a Goddess group, and a children's group (if children are present). The God and Goddess groups can be divided randomly, by personal choice, or by gender. The children, depending on their ages, may need an adult with them. Often teenagers will happily supervise the children.

Explain these groups will be now be working to create an enactment representing some of the themes of Lammas. The enactments can utilize song, movement, theatre, talking, dance, mime, or anything else they can think of. The groups will have about twenty minutes to half an hour to create their enactments, which should be about two to five minutes long.

The God group should:
- Discuss death; how they feel about death, the times they have felt death came close to them, symbolic or actual

- Discuss how this is relevant to the themes and time of Lammas

- Create a ritual enactment that expresses death within the seasonal context

The Goddess group should:
- Discuss mourning; what they have mourned for in their lives and what mourning is like for them

- Discuss how this is relevant to the themes and time of Lammas

- Create a ritual enactment that expresses mourning within the seasonal context

The children's group should:
- Talk about seeds, what they do, and what they mean

- Talk about different types of seeds

- Create an enactment about the promise of the seeds that are saved from the harvest for next year's planting. They can present this as a play, song, or dance, or use elements of all three

Each group then presents their enactment to the whole group in the order of God group, Goddess group, and Children's group. Each group can ask the others to sit and watch, stand around them in a circle, or to participate, following instructions.

7. Raising Energy

Begin singing the song at the completion of the enactments. If you have a drummer or percussionist, that person can lead into the song by beginning with the beat. Start quietly, reminding others of the words and tune and gradually increase the energy of the song. Turn it into a round if you like.

This is the time to raise energy if you are going to do so. You may also choose to have a spiral dance or some other form of dance.

At the conclusion bring out the loaf of bread you baked. I like to have it carried out by a young man. Have someone speak a blessing over it—of the grain that has been cut, the energy that went into making the bread, and the symbolism of eating a piece. A sample blessing is, *I bless this bread that holds the life of the Grain God within it. We thank him for his life, his energy that nurtures our lives, and for his part in the ever-turning cycle of life.*

The person carrying the bread should then offer it around so everyone can break off a piece and eat it.

8. Making the Lammas Dolly

This activity is fully described on page 215, immediately after the ritual

Explain the group is going to create a Lammas Dolly with this seasonal magic bound into it.

The Lammas Dolly may become a life-sized human figure, a smaller figure of a man, a circle bisected with spokes of a wheel, a peace symbol, or a quartered circle. I find it best to let the shape arise from those making it and from the materials available rather than giving specific instructions as to how it will look. You can use ribbon or string where and if necessary (stalks of grass can also be used to bind).

The Lammas Dolly can be placed on the altar or hung on a wall. If you keep it for six months until Imbolc, it can be taken outside and gifted to the earth, as a symbol of seeds that have been saved from the harvest until the new planting time.

9. Complete the Ritual

You may like to sing the song through a final few times, as everyone stands around and admires the Lammas Dolly.

Honor and thank all those invoked, acknowledge the directions and elements in the reverse order that they were called, and dissolve the circle. Generally the same people who did the calling and casting do this.

- **Acknowledge:** The power of seeds is thanked, the Grain God is thanked, and the Earth Goddess is thanked.

- **Acknowledge the directions and elements:**

Northern Hemisphere:
Below and Above

Northwest	Water and earth	Seeds saved, storehouses, fallow fields
Southwest	Fire and water	Ripening, fruit forming, harvest
Southeast	Air and fire	Saplings, buds, grain growing
Northeast	Earth and air	First sprouts of new growth

Southern Hemisphere:
Below and Above

Southwest	Water and earth	Seeds saved, storehouses, fallow fields
Northwest	Fire and water	Ripening; fruit forming, harvest
Northeast	Air and fire	Saplings, buds, grain growing
Southeast	Earth and air	First sprouts of new growth

- **Dissolve the circle:** If a circle was cast, the same person walks around it in the opposite direction gathering up the energy or otherwise dispersing it. If you sprinkled flour on a floor, sweep it up; if flour was sprinkled outside, it may already be lost in the grass or earth, but you could symbolically sweep or rake it away.

Thank each person for coming and for the energy they have contributed and begin the Lammas Feast if you are having one.

Lammas Activity:
Lammas Dolly

Making a Lammas Dolly is fun to do with children as a stand-alone ritual. The gathering and choosing of the grain can become part of the activity, setting out together into the garden or a wild piece of park with pruning shears and a basket. Each child can choose some grasses or seedpods they especially like (try to make sure they leave as much stem as possible on their grain for easier incorporation into the dolly).

Alternatively, this ritual can be done solo as your offering for the season. The Lammas Dolly can also be incorporated into a larger ritual with a group of people working together to create it.

Although it is commonly known as a *corn dolly*, in many places corn (or more often barley or wheat) may not be available. In Australia we've used a mix of long-stemmed grasses and rushes with foliage from native shrubs that produce seeds at the ends of long stalks added in for variety. Someone always brings a few brightly colored weeds. We also get offerings of corn cobs (sometimes with a stalk), sunflowers, and parsley or other things from the vegetable patch that have gone to seed.

You will need:

- Grasses with long stems and/or wheat or barley on the stalk. It's lovely if everyone brings some of the grain

- Other grain-on-the-stalk such as sunflowers, corn on the cob, other seeding plants (optional)

- Scissors or pruning shears for collecting and trimming

- Wool, ribbon, or string (optional but helpful)

Time:

- 30 minutes to make the dolly, or longer if you incorporate gathering the grain into the ritual

Intention

The intention for a Lammas Dolly is usually to bless the harvest and thank the grain itself. You may wish to make this more particular, blessing a project you are working on and thanking your tools and any aspect of divinity you feel is assisting.

Method

Sit around on the floor in a circle or around a largish table, depending on the size of your group and amount of materials.

- Introduce the theme of Lammas and the tradition of making a dolly from the first part of the harvest. This had several meanings: as ritually preserving the first sacred stalks harvested for the God (whose body they literally were) as well as symbolically saving some of the seed for the next planting. If the dolly is made into a figure (rather than a geometric shape), there is a further symbolic inference that the Grain God himself is being preserved within that shape. He is the one who will bless the rest of the harvest.

• Explain you want the group to create a Lammas Dolly with some of this seasonal magic bound or woven into it. Ask everyone to introduce themselves and offer their grain or whatever they have brought and place it in the center of the table or floor. This is a messy undertaking so you may wish to lay down an old cloth or newspaper first.

• Each person can say why they chose this particular grain and what it means to them or offer a blessing to go with it; all these attributes can be woven into the dolly. You might say such things as, *I chose a sunflower because sunflowers make me feel happy, I bring this thistle and its blessing of courage,* or *I offer this grass in memory of the Grain God.*

• Now begin making the dolly. Often one or two people will start organizing things, suggesting a shape or theme for the dolly. The Lammas Dolly may become a life-sized human figure or a smaller figure that can stand or be displayed; sometimes the dolly is a hollow man who can have wishes and blessings in the form of flowers placed inside him; sometimes a circle bisected with spokes of a wheel or another shape. Let the shape arise from those making it and from the materials available. You can use ribbon or string where necessary (stalks of grass can also be used to bind).

• Sometimes the shape is roughly laid out first and is followed by the binding, weaving, and plaiting; sometimes it is more spontaneous. I've never had the process not result in a dolly at the end. If there are children, they will often play a key role in the craft aspects.

• The Lammas Dolly can be placed on the altar or hung on a wall. If you save it for six months, at Imbolc it can be taken outside and gifted to the earth as a symbol of seeds that have been saved from the harvest until the new planting time.

Autumn Equinox

*Celebrated on or close to September 21 in the Northern Hemisphere
and March 21 in the Southern Hemisphere.*

Autumn Equinox

The Autumn Equinox is the first Festival I remember Damon taking charge of. He was four and he insisted we go to the supermarket first thing in the morning. We went and he selected fruit to some inner vision; he wanted a wreath, so we wove one with the dark green leaves and brilliant yellow of wattle. I have a photo of him in the garden, kneeling in front of his miniature chair that had turned into a fruit-filled altar, the wreath slipping a little with his hair over his eyes, earnestly engaged in ritual.

He knew what to do at the Autumn Equinox. Build an altar. Make it beautiful with the fruits of the harvest. Wear a flowery wreath. He held a private ritual; I couldn't tell whether he was thanking the Goddess or creating some special four-year-old magic. Observing him, I thought there was nothing in the way between him and ritual; not like adults who battle varying levels of uncertainty, a hundred competing demands, and general laziness. If I said it was the Autumn Equinox to Damon, then immediately the moment of ritual was upon us. It was like our ritual was the one that kept the Wheel turning; without our celebration, the equinox wouldn't really have happened. It was not abstract for him—a discussion of days and nights of equal length, a turning toward winter and going within—it was concrete. Fruit, altar, and flowers.

The Autumn Equinox is often celebrated as a Harvest Festival with country fairs and church altars covered in produce. These represent gratitude for the accumulated wealth of summer and a time to recall an era when if your storehouse and cellar weren't stocked full you might not make it through winter. Both equinoxes have days and nights of equal length, but where spring tips into growth and light, autumn tips into the season of death. The Autumn Equinox is associated with balance, thanksgiving, and the turning into the dark. Anticipating the future deprivations of winter adds to the gaiety of the Harvest Festival that turns into a celebration of life, splendid in decoration and revels.

In both the Southern and Northern Hemispheres, the Autumn Equinox is aligned with the west. Mythically speaking, the west has long been associated with dreams, mystery, and journeying; especially to mysterious and unknown lands, including even the lands of death and the apple isle of Avalon. In most magical and many Pagan traditions, the element of the west is water. The most famous symbol of water is the chalice. Like a cauldron, the chalice is seen as a womb, holding the waters of life and a variable promise of plenty, transformation, occult knowledge, the blessing of the Goddess, or the fulfillment of desire if one is lucky enough to be offered a drink from it.

In any small tribe or relatively isolated village, harvest time brings a clear idea of whether or not there are resources to survive the coming season. They would be choosing livestock, calculating which were worth looking after through winter and which should be slaughtered now at their fattest. Similarly, we can use this time to ask ourselves which of our projects and endeavors we should complete or sign off on. Some may be projects we consider failures and not worth putting any more energy into, where others are successfully completed. As we lay them aside, perhaps we will even remember to give ourselves the traditional rest between completion and a new beginning, so we are not just rushing heedlessly on but allowing each thing its own period of gestation and birthing.

These moments of balance and of pausing between one state and another are offered to us at the equinoxes. It is up to us to recognize them and make them meaningful in our lives. We can ask ourselves, *Where do I need balance? Do I spend too long sitting at a desk, and not enough time in the garden, doing what I love, playing with the kids, or adventuring into the wild? Do I have a balanced diet? Do I balance my own needs with those of my family? Is my spiritual practice balanced?* If I ask myself these questions and it seems glaringly obvious that my life is not balanced, do I dare take some time out, and try to bring balance?

Autumn Equinox Memoir

Mist rises up in great swathes out of the gully and floats toward the house, embracing it and drifting past. Showers of rain descend intermittently. There's been a change in the season; we have to light the fire. It's the kind of weather people don't feel like coming out in, they might not make it out of their own living rooms to a ritual a long way up the hill. But that doesn't stop us. Over the years we've done rituals with ten, twenty, or thirty people, or sometimes just four or five. This afternoon, eight people show up. It feels tight—special, magical—that we are the ones who ignore the weather and external events to pursue our celebration no matter what. Even that we recognize this inclement weather as sacred, exactly what is due for this Festival.

We cast the circle into four quarters and Damon, a teenager, calls to the center. We have a harvest altar and a table laid with a feast. My silver moon bowl is filled with beautiful objects representing light and summer: crystals, shells, and birds' feathers. Because the weather only changed so recently, we've also been able to find frangipani flowers, their fleshy white petals giving way to splashes of yellow where the petals whorl out, solid with summery perfume. The Autumn Equinox is not just about balance but about crossing the line that bisects the circle, equinox to equinox, leaving summer behind to head into the dark. I always look forward to this crossing, at least a little. Samhain is the time of my birthday, so it feels like I am gifted that part of the year, darkness with its mysteries, anguish, and beauties; once I start heading into that quadrant of the circle, I'm going home.

It's a strange mixture, the Autumn Equinox; all that imagery of the west's setting sun, beckoning journeys, and dreaming coupled with the solidness of the year's achievements, harvest, and balance. It makes the theme of crossing over even stronger that this Festival straddles the material and spirit worlds so convincingly.

I feel between those two worlds myself. Here we are, a small, intent circle of people creating an ordered ritual inside my house and yet outside the mist swirls and beckons. Here we are, with summer ended and something else moving onto the land so suddenly, so convincingly that we have frangipanis on the same day we have to light a fire to keep warm. Here we are, celebrating our harvest in the earthly realm while crossing over into the numinous realm of mists and mysteries. Here I am—a mother, keeper of a house and land, guardian of a circle—and yet, here I am, dreamer and seeker, always yearning into the insubstantial realms of writing, myth, and the search for love.

In our own magical group, the Circle of Eight, we move each new moon into the next of the eight directions around the Wheel, and because this Autumn Equinox ritual has fallen on the new moon we're shifting tonight, during the ritual. It happens that I'm shifting from the west, the direction of the Autumn Equinox, into the southwest, the Southern Hemisphere place of Samhain. I'm turning exactly with the Wheel of the Year; it happens occasionally, but not very often so perfectly like this. Not often enough to make it an ordinary event. One way or another I have an anticipation that's not common for the Autumn Equinox; more usually it is a bright celebration against a backdrop of looming uncertainty.

In our ritual we do all the usual things. Damon leads some warm-up games he's enamored of, then we talk about what the Autumn Equinox means to us. We learn a song. We move on to our individual harvests, making offerings to the altar. People offer vegetables they've grown, school assignments completed, symbols of spiritual practice.

I have a woven strand of native bushes from my garden, which I've tended painstakingly over the last five years. Most days I've spent an hour weeding, clearing, digging, mulching, and caring for the hundreds upon hundreds of lomandra, bangalow palms, native ginger, cordyline, dianella, sedge, river lily, birds' nest ferns, low-spreading ground covers, and flowering natives I've planted. It's been a labor of desperation as I struggle to maintain any grip at all on this huge property and this vast house that contains only Damon and me. This life I'm living that is a bit too much for me. This braid is a symbol of my hard work, of brokering a deal with the wilderness and weeds and overwhelm; I hope placing it on the altar might mean I'm crossing the line.

We have done these things so often, I have been through these rituals so many times, it no longer feels like I am moving around the Wheel at all, but instead it is moving through me. I think of it as a great three- or four-dimensional wheel of light, starlight; a thick core of sparking, living, silver-white light that spins and spits and turns; the galaxies in their black night and I don't so much progress around the edge of it as merge through its layers, sensing its shifts and balances as if they were part of me. Although my presence might hover near one point rather than another at any given time, I feel the entirety of it. I am like those particles that, unobserved, are everywhere at once; until they suddenly have to be on record, when they settle on the most likely point. Between observations they exist thinly spread and everywhere throughout the whole. I am both particle and wave, as the Wheel is endless and all and simultaneous, yet somehow can be recognized, pinned down, and called the Autumn Equinox at this moment, in this hemisphere, in this house, and during this ritual.

We talk of light and dark and the moment of balance. We choose a partner and explain where we are with that balance in our own lives; even though I speak my struggles of overwhelm and loneliness, words can't express the strength of my feelings which are so visceral, so knotted into my tendons and dreaming that I live on the edge of the worlds, half in my head at least but still trying to hold on to this world, raising a son and keeping the land in check and the house together. And I'm lonely. Once I had a bright and beautiful relationship, but it's long gone and I've tried now for many years to learn to be all of it, to hold both sides inside myself.

Damon brings around the moon bowl so each of us can choose an item from it to carry with us into the darkness. I choose a frangipani, reminder of the white-and-gold part of the year, and the potential of love. We sing our song, gathering threads of light through the chant and our voices weave them stronger and stronger. When it dies away, I step forward and drag a piece of chalk east to west through the circle across the floor, and our song switches into the dark; no words now, just sound rising and rising in groans and growls and booming, strong voices. It's dusk and we haven't turned the lights on. The fire is lit, but it's behind the bright half of the circle, and we all take a step back so the circle is empty of everything except its chalk line which meets our altar in the west, and we watch the looming dark beyond, through the windows.

Will you carry light forward, from this half of the year? Will you be the light in the dark? I call my questions out, interposing them in quieter moments of the chant, shouting them through the sound waves of mounting dark. I twirl my frangipani in my fingers and it seems a big ask, to let this little flower guide me into the night, the winter, the dark time of mystery and going within. It's against all evidence, really, that one should feel hope at this time of the year.

Although we're a small group, the sound is loud and confident. Our task is to continue sounding the darkness while one by one we step forward, from the light half of the circle and cross the line into the dark, carrying our symbol, our own light with us. This is all experimental, in flux, but it seems to be working and I am wide awake now—the ritual has come alive. They are heartbreaking, these single figures stepping forward bravely into the gloom, stepping toward the growing darkness outside the windows, holding out a single flower or crystal or shell as a talisman, trying to sing their light against the huge sound we're making. And yet they don't waver, they don't crash or give way, they walk across the line as if it were not just a challenge but personal necessity and move into the shadows.

As soon as I step forward of the others and inside the circle, even though I can hear the huge sound they're making, it doesn't seem important. My flower seems important, and the other half of the circle where I am headed, but all that noise behind me is merely background. I start sounding out for myself— not dark this time, but light—a small thread of singing against this backdrop of drowning sound. I count my riches, my harvest. There's my son, singing behind me, and my whole circle, singing me forward into the dark. There's the house and land I've struggled with, but it's ours, shelter and more than shelter; a place that welcomes friends and rituals and feasts, and the beauty of the land is its own thing; those swooping flocks of birds in the day, the fig trees, the gullies and the stream that flows when there's a downpour, the views of cliffs and trees, the clear air and lush fertility of it all, and these deep mists that creep up from the valley. I have my writing, my traveling, I'm doing my work and feel alive and challenged and deeply rewarded in it. I am absolutely rich.

I'm also turning with the Wheel, cresting with the new moon as it sinks westward. I head into my next position for the Circle of Eight, the place of Samhain, as it beckons the year toward it, opening its mouth and swallowing up the remnants of summer, whatever might be left. Me and my frangipani. I'm heading down toward the realms of the Dark Goddess and surely I know her better than I know anything else; my steps are confident and that little flower I hold is exactly like a beacon, a memory of summer that will guide me through the unknown. I remember standing in the heart of the mysteries, I remember what it's like to look into the eyes of the Dark Goddess and see myself reflected back, I remember what it is to love and be loved, and to give oneself over, utterly, to the turning of the Wheel.

My breath gets stronger and my voice louder; then I open my mouth and really let it out, this song brewing in my guts, this shining, singing sound that is high and clear and cuts into darkness like a knife, like a bell, like a breath of wind and then it is so loud, my own sound in my ears, that I can't really hear anything else and it lifts me and I walk forward on it, over the line and into the dark and I could keep walking forever really, singing this song which is my own, singing my light into the darkness. It is not scary, bad, or dire; it's beautiful and I am enraptured by it, entranced by the ease and grace. It doesn't feel like I'm entering the Underworld, tombs of darkness, or anything like that. It's like approaching fairyland, the mysterious other world that lies next to ours, glimmering but largely unseen by mortals. The flower and I are the light and that's enough.

I tell myself the real dark is much stronger than this, but it doesn't seem to matter. When I finally have to stop making this sound and draw breath, I turn around to face the others. Everything is transformed from this side of the circle. When I look back at them they are lit up from behind, by the flames in the fireplace. They are creatures of light, shining, but their faces in shadow; whereas I stand with the dark at my back and look toward the light. This is so fundamental; of course I know this about light and dark, but to actually discover it from inside a ritual rewrites it as revelation. In this moment, I know how it feels, embodied, that standing in the light you must look at the dark, but standing in the dark it's the light you're looking at.

Damon follows me through and I feel only proud of him, victorious that he too will discover this marvelous thing of carrying the light and how one becomes it. Then everything is transformed. The Autumn Equinox. At this moment of crossing into the dark the balance is struck, not just in the Wheel that's halfway between summer and winter, but inside, in the knowledge of self, where the light is experienced exactly because of the dark. I venture and venture into what calls me; the realms of the Goddess, of ritual, and myth, of singing the spells of the land and my own imagination as I turn in spirals and labyrinthine patterns inward and inward; and you could say it is into the dark, carrying my light with me. And when I turn back, I bring the darkness with me as a cloak, an embrace, like dark wings. I watch Damon's face, shadowed until he reaches the depths of dark beside me and turns around, and then he is all lit up.

Balance and Foreknowledge

Autumn is said by many to be the most beautiful season. The sun is still warm but without the blasting heat of summer, there's a nip in the air or a cool breeze with earlier, crisp nights, reminding us of what's to come. There's a sense of purpose as people rush about; once they would have been concentrating on getting harvests in from the fields, but now they are swinging into the serious gear of getting the work year under way, summer holidays forgotten.

We've often used the theme of *crossing* in our Autumn Equinox rituals; crossing from one realm to another, crossing from one half of the year to the next, crossing from light into darkness, or summer into winter. We've passed through gateways or leapt across a line or progressed from the light half of the circle filled with tea lights into the dark half. One time Cathryn stood at the western doorway holding a shell and each person whispered what they longed for into the shell as they passed by her and out the door.

Sometimes we've asked people to call out a single word, recognizing or invoking something they needed for balance as they crossed over. I clearly remember Damon as an eleven-year-old crossing the Autumn Equinox line and calling out, *Courage!* as he went through. It seemed symbolic that he was walking away from me, and I ached for him. Over the next couple of months he underwent three tests of courage, not set by anyone, but just his interpretation of the circumstances of his life. First he met the challenge of staying in his own bed during a thunderstorm. Next came the challenge of standing up to someone he was afraid of. And finally he took a flight as an unaccompanied child from Melbourne to San Francisco. It's an eighteen-hour flight; it was the first international trip he had ever done by himself; and after 9/11 he was particularly wary of setting foot in America again. When I met him in the San Francisco airport, we agreed that lone trip crossing hemispheres and the international dateline acknowledged his courage, and that now he had earned what he'd invoked three and a half months earlier.

Falling between the first death of Lammas, with the beginning of the grain harvest and the dying of the year at Samhain submersed in death, the Autumn Equinox still doesn't seem particularly dire. Perhaps the stability of being a solidly balanced Quarter Festival rather than a slippery in-between Cross-Quarter makes a difference, but I always feel I have arrived somewhere when it's the Autumn Equinox. The harvest is traditionally a time of assessment, leading us to reflect on what we have or have not achieved. It's the time of accounting. When the grain is stacked in the storehouses and the tithes are paid, we know whether we're in for a slim winter, perhaps barely scraping through, or whether our harvest will easily be able to feed us and our loved ones.

These themes very clearly translate into modern life. Have we achieved what we set out to do? Can we sufficiently provide for those who are dependent on us? And are we satisfied with our harvest this time around? Even tithing—the practice of giving one-tenth of one's harvest (or earnings) to the Church or to charity—seems appropriate; have we given generously and sufficiently? If we answer these questions in the negative, this Festival is the time to make good the balance. Give your offerings, celebrate what you have, and do what needs to be done to create a balance.

Immediately after this brief moment of the equinox we cross the line. We move from the bright, light-filled part of the year, and perhaps of ourselves, to the inner, shadowy realm. There we have the opportunity to journey deeply within ourselves, passing through Samhain and letting go of the old, and then—possibly after a period of nothingness, waiting, or not-knowing— experience inevitable rebirth with the Winter Solstice. So the Wheel leads us, step by step, on its own circular and endless journey. At the Autumn Equinox, as during the American harvest festival of Thanksgiving, it's appropriate to concentrate on what we are blessed with and have achieved; whatever that may be.

This is to come to a balance within ourselves, a reckoning where we acknowledge all we've received and the harvest we've brought in, and then also look at what or where we are lacking, how we may feel we have failed ourselves or others (perhaps in spite of much struggle), and how we may not be living up to our deeper dreams and wishes. This meditation may fall naturally into two halves; that of the material world and the spiritual. So we can look at our harvest in the world and also our harvest within. We can use this moment of balance to focus on how and where our inward journey will take us. This is a crossing over from the light into the dark, from the known into the realms of mystery, and from the outward focus of summer to the inward focus of winter. It's a moment when one's life can be weighed up, balanced, and a choice made—a step taken forward.

Many of the Festivals have what appear to be contradictory themes that pull both ways at once. The utter darkness coupled with rebirth at Winter Solstice is one of these, and the Autumn Equinox is another. In the midst of plenty, we dream of death. That is, all around us are the fruits of our harvest, our fullness, and our completion; yet our minds turn toward winter, scarcity, and inevitable death. Perhaps it is not so contradictory when we associate more strongly with the natural world; the vegetables and fruits have died, to be harvested and placed on our altars and in our cellars. Their death is our plenty. Those of us who have European trees around will notice them in their seasonal death phase, shifting form as they prepare for winter. Livestock is traditionally culled around this time and the length of each day continues to shorten. Death and plenty live side by side, hand in hand.

Autumn Equinox is a moment of recognition as well. When we look at our grown children and realize that although we may not have given them the perfect childhood, they are already becoming independent and moving into the world. We look at our relationship, our single state, or our community and realize that although it may not be everything we dreamed of (and what did we really know, when we had those dreams?), it is something real and tangible we have created that continues to support and sustain us. When we look at the entire cycle as the length of a human life, the Autumn Equinox equates with that time around turning sixty when we are both assessing all the work we have done and asking ourselves what comes next, what we will do with our remaining time.

We may also look at something in our lives regardless of our age—and this can be a relationship, a job, an addiction, or spiritual path—and realize it is toxic. We have given to it, poured many resources, given care, and even given love to the situation, yet it does not nurture us; we cannot grow within it, and perhaps we even feel it threatens to destroy us. Autumn is a good time for culling. For completion. It is just before the time of year when there's no choice but to let go. At the Autumn Equinox we can choose to step aside from what we're finished with, or what does not serve us—acknowledging, letting go, and walking freely into another part of our lives. It's about being ready to face the dark in every possible way. Ready because of the full storehouses, ready because we've found internal balance, ready because we're willing to step over the line.

Once I made a beautiful altar, filled with precious things—candles, colored leaves, special little statues—and left one half of it completely empty. Half was lush and vibrant and half was plain brick with not even a cloth. I meant it to depict my life; not that my life was empty, for I had my work, my son, my friends, and my house, all of which was represented in the full half of the altar. But I also meant to make room for what I wished—for my life to hold an empty space rather than be entirely cluttered up with myself until there was no room for relationship. I wanted to give it room to exist on its own.

Acknowledging both halves of life and of the year leaves us room to move from one to another, to experience both. It was at an Autumn Equinox ritual that my friend and I stood back to back in the center of the circle and invoked the Light and Dark Goddesses. She wore red and stood facing the fire quarter, and I was all in black looking toward earth. We stretched our arms out, hands pointing east and west along the dividing line of the circle; she called to summer and warmth and light and love and I called out to winter, to the dark and sheltering of night and the mysteries.

She danced about the circle, kissing people and blessing them; I waited, still and silent, knowing the time was mine, and hers was past as of this day when the year swings into dark. So I let her dance and sing and kiss and then I called out, a long screaming twist of sound that went on and on and I bent and grabbed the saucer of charcoal paint I'd made earlier and smeared a great handful of it across my face, over my hand and up my arm. I advanced on the circle, stalking them, rushing them, and they flinched backward or put an arm about their children or faced me bravely and I placed my hand against their faces, one by one, leaving black marks behind. I looked them in the eye, I challenged them, beckoned to them.

Then we stood back to back again and slowly turned, inviting them to see that we are one, that summer turns to winter turns to summer always and always. The two faces of the Goddess, light and dark, are two faces of her; she is always with us, ahead of us, and beside us, and we are ever in her embrace. To acknowledge one side only is to know only half, to be willingly blind. The two in one is her mystery, just as is the pregnant mother, the earth waiting for spring to give forth life from new seeds, the lovers entwined together, or dying into the arms of death. Two in one and all our knowledge and love of the brightness and joy of life leads inevitably here, to this day and this step to cross the line and walk into darkness.

We celebrate the harvest, we stand in a moment of balance, and we cross into the dark. Autumn Equinox. In the midst of plenty, we dream of death and all is held within the embrace of the Wheel.

Autumn Equinox Ritual

Notes: "Ritual Basics" on page 295 covers many aspects of ritual, including grounding, casting circles, invocations, and participation.

Instructions for making the Autumn Altar exist more fully on page 249. Section 8, "Crossing into the Dark" is the central part of this ritual.

Ask everyone to bring:

- Items from nature for the Autumn Altar from their flower gardens, vegetable gardens, herb gardens, or small natural items they have found (for example, feathers, colored leaves, pretty stones)

- A gift for the altar, whether this is a colored altar cloth, a candle, or a decorative item

- A symbol or piece of a completed project they have been working on (for example, the title page of a book, a piece of wood from a newly built house, or a memento representing a relationship)

- Food for the Autumn Feast, if you are having one

Other things needed for this ritual:

- An altar; depending how many people you are expecting, you may want to make this multilayered and constructed with planks and bricks, crates, or boxes. You can build this altar in the west (the direction aligned with the Autumn Equinox in both hemispheres) or in the center of your circle. You can also build it during the ritual

- Chalk, ribbon, or some other visible way to make a division of the circle partway through the ritual

- A beautiful bowl or dish holding flowers, tea lights, or other symbols of light

- Chimes or a gong are very useful during the walking meditation

- Drum/percussion instrument (one or more)

Clothing suggestion:

- Autumnal colors; alternatively, wear your richest and most elaborate clothing to celebrate the richness of harvest

Roles in ritual:

These can all be done by different people or one or two people can take all or most of the roles depending on how confident and experienced the group is:

- Casting the circle and calling directions; this can be done by several different people or all by one person

- Grounding

- Leading warm-ups

- Leading discussion and giving instructions

- Timekeeper (this may not be necessary, or can be combined with another role)

- Drummer/song leader

Length of Ritual: 1–1.5 hours

Ritual

1. Gathering

Welcome the group to the ritual space and take care of any housekeeping. If some people are unfamiliar with ritual etiquette, briefly explain how you'd like the ritual to run.

Announce the intention of the ritual. For example, *Today we're having a ritual to celebrate the Autumn Equinox and our harvest, On this day we acknowledge dark and light as equals,* or *We stand at one of the balancing points as we turn away from summer to the inward half of the year.*

Ask everyone to introduce themselves briefly. Start with yourself, to give a demonstration of the type of introduction you want. If you have a large group (over twenty), you can ask people simply to introduce themselves to the person or people next to them.

2. Grounding and Warm-ups

Warm-ups are optional, but are great in a group that doesn't know each other well, isn't practiced in ritual, or when children are present.

GROUNDING:

- Briefly introduce the idea of grounding; that it is done to assist everyone to become more present, feel alive in their bodies, and release any distractions.

- Offer a world tree grounding, sending roots into the earth and branches out to the sky. Once this is established, ask each person to feel into the balance between earth and sky in themselves, between grounding roots and stretching branches.

- Speak slowly and clearly, adding intonation and variety to your voice to assist and inspire those listening.

- Finish with a clear instruction for everyone to open their eyes (if they were shut) and become fully present.

Suggested Warm-ups:

- **Physical:** Balancing bodies; ask everyone to find someone of similar height and weight and experiment with different ways of balancing themselves. At the end, ask each pair to demonstrate one of their balancing positions.

- **Vocal:** Balancing voices; after some initial sounding and voice warm-ups, ask half the circle to make a summer sound and the other half to create a winter sound. Try working with both sounds at once, playing with rising and falling to make patterns.

3. Creating a Sacred Space

- **Cast a circle:** If you want to give your circle casting a particularly autumnal flavor, scatter autumn leaves around the edge of your circle. Otherwise, have someone walk around the perimeter of your circle using their hand or a magical tool to draw the outline of the circle.

- **Call to the directions and the elements:** Have four people each call to one direction and then together call Above and Below. You can have two men and two women. Alternatively, it can all be done by one person.

Northern Hemisphere:

East	Air	Sunrise, the moment of balance that swings into light
South	Fire	Midday sun, the extreme of light
West	Water	Sunset, Autumn Equinox, and the moment of balance that swings into darkness
North	Earth	Night, the extreme of dark
Above and Below		

Southern Hemisphere:

East	Air	Sunrise, the moment of balance that swings into light
North	Fire	Midday sun, the extreme of light
West	Water	Sunset, Autumn Equinox, and the moment of balance that swings into darkness
South	Earth	Night, the extreme of dark
Above and Below		

4. Introducing the Autumn Equinox

Explain the Autumn Equinox is one of two days of the year when night and day are of equal length, midway between the two solstices. You might mention that in the other hemisphere it is the Spring Equinox, the other day of balance. Thus, the whole earth is in balance on this day. Autumn Equinox is often associated with the harvest whether it has been successful or disappointing. The traditional harvest feast represents bounty and the hope that this harvest will be enough to last through winter. Both equinoxes are excellent moments for assessing balance within our lives; whether that is a classic work–life balance or another balance, such as balancing our diets or balancing our care for ourselves with our care for others.

After the initial explanation, ask each person to contribute their own ideas about what the Autumn Equinox or this time of year means to them and where they live. It may mean a change in the weather, time to settle down to a year of schooling or work, or time to prepare for winter. If it is a large group (over twenty people), you may need to break into smaller groups for this section.

You might also wish to discuss the aspect of the Autumn Equinox as a balancing time, whether people feel balanced or unbalanced. Bringing this theme into our personal lives can be done in a second round of the sharing to deepen each person's relationship to the Festival and the ritual.

5. Creating the Autumn Altar

This activity is described fully on page 249, immediately after the ritual.

Ask everyone to bring all their altar items into the circle except for the symbol of their completed project; with these items, everyone can create the altar spontaneously and all together. This results in a more themed altar (for example, all the pumpkins may be grouped together) than if each person just does their own thing one at a time.

Once the altar is constructed, move back into a circle and include the altar either inside the circle or on the western edge. Ask each person to step forward to name their project and the piece of it they've brought, then have them place their pieces on the altar either among everything else or on a special part of the altar designated for these projects.

6. Learning the Chant

Introduce the chant or chants you will be using later in the ritual. There are many chants on CDs, online, and in songbooks. You may already have favorite chants that are well-known to your group. You might also have a songwriter among you. Choose a simple song or chant that is true to the themes of your ritual and teach it to the group by singing it a couple of times and then teaching it line by line. It's useful to sing it through together at least eight or ten times, so when you begin singing later in the ritual everyone can easily join in without being having to be reminded of the words or tune.

7. Darkness and Light Meditation

This is a walking meditation. The facilitator stands in the center to give guidance and instructions, while everyone else slowly walks (beyond the strict confines of the circle, to give themselves room, but within hearing). It helps to have some chimes or a gong to work with.

Ask everyone to begin moving about the space slowly and meditatively, weaving a pattern among each other. They should gaze mainly downward, keeping just enough attention on the outside world to avoid bumping into others. They should breathe consciously and send most of their awareness inward. When the facilitator sounds the chime or gong, everyone stops, finds a partner, and speaks with their partner according to the instructions that are given. On the second sounding of the chime or gong, they continue moving. The facilitator should speak a lead-in of at least a few sentences before asking each question.

There are three questions, spaced out from each other, with the answers spoken each time to different partners.

- In what area of your life or yourself is the light strongest?

- In what area of your life or yourself is the darkness strongest?

- Where and how do you seek balance in your life between the dark and light?

8. Crossing into the Dark

This directly follows the walking meditation, so move smoothly into this part of the ritual.

Once the gong or chimes sound to signify the completion of the third question, draw an east-to-west line across your circle. Use chalk, a ribbon, rope, or some other form of line that can be clearly seen.

Have someone take the bowl with objects of light around for everyone to choose one. Explain each person will now cross over into the darkened part of the year, taking their light with them, as the Wheel itself swings around to that part of the circle on this day. It is an opportunity to address any balance they wish to bring into their lives as well as acceptance and recognition of the dark.

Ask everyone to step back to the edges of the circle and begin a group tone to represent winter, or the darkened half of the circle.

If possible, retain light over the light half of the circle (the southern side if you are in the Northern Hemisphere or the northern side if you are in the Southern Hemisphere) and leave the dark half of the circle shadowed. At the very least, make sure there are no lit candles or other lights in your dark half.

Each person takes a turn and stands forward into the light half of the circle, gathering their own light within them. They may choose to do this with a sound, a gesture, or internally. The rest of the group begins intoning for the winter, darkness, stillness, and inwardness; within this soundscape, the person in the center moves toward and over the division in the circle, into the dark half. They may make a gesture, shout, or sound to halt or change the general toning; they may join in with it; or they may wait for it to die down of itself. Then they rejoin the circle and it is the next person's turn.

Sharing how this moment was for each person is a wonderful discussion to have over your Autumn Feast, or to privately check in with the ritual participants afterward. You may choose to add a discussion or feedback session into the ritual.

9. Raising Energy

The drummer, percussionist, or song leader should begin as soon as the last person has crossed through the circle, picking up on the energy and transforming it into the direction of the song. Begin singing clearly so others have help remembering the words and realize where you are taking the ritual. Some rituals will have many drummers or one or two great singers; other rituals will rely on collaborative group effort.

You may choose to raise a cone of power, or just to experience the song or chant fully and then drop it down to the ground in keeping with the earth energy of the darker half of the year.

10. Complete the Ritual

Acknowledge the directions and elements in the reverse order that they were called and dissolve the circle. Generally the same people who did the calling and casting do this.

- **Acknowledge the directions and elements:**

Northern Hemisphere:
Below and Above

North	Earth	Night, the extreme of dark
West	Water	Sunset, Autumn Equinox, and the moment of balance that swings into darkness
South	Fire	Midday sun, the extreme of light
East	Air	Sunrise, the moment of balance that swings into light

Southern Hemisphere:
Below and Above

South	Earth	Night, the extreme of dark
West	Water	Sunset, Autumn Equinox, and the moment of balance that swings into darkness
North	Fire	Midday sun, the extreme of light
East	Air	Sunrise, the moment of balance that swings into light

- **Release the circle:** If a circle was cast, the same person walks around it in the opposite direction, gathering up the energy or otherwise dispersing it. If you put autumn leaves around the outside of the circle, gather them, sweep them away, or just leave them to decompose into the earth if you are outside.

Thank each person for coming and for the energy they have contributed. Extinguish candles as needed. If you are having an Autumn Feast, begin it now, leaving the Autumn Altar at least for the duration of the Feast.

Autumn Equinox
Activity: Autumn Altar

You can create an Autumn Altar on its own, indoors or outdoors, or as part of a larger ritual. It's a great thing to do with your family, but it can easily be done on your own. If you make (and leave) your altar outside, make sure nothing on it could be poisonous or dangerous to wildlife. Altars can be as creative as you are; you could hang one from the branches of a tree, build it around the base of a birdbath, or create a tiny, fairy-sized one nestled under some bushes.

The emphasis for the Autumn Altar is the harvest of the year—what you have grown, learned, and achieved; what you have received in your life; and what you are thankful for. There will be material things you have worked for, such as a job, garden, house, or creative or business venture. There will be relationships into which you have put time and care. There may be a spiritual path you've been following and growth or understanding you've experienced. There may be political, community, or world-scale issues you've cared about, contributed to, or fought for. Many of these things will not be completed, but you can still acknowledge and give thanks for what they've brought you.

Children may also want to add beautiful or shiny or loved things to the altar. A year can be a long time for a small child to reflect on—try to give them some markers to work with when you're encouraging them to discover what it is they've achieved during the last twelve months; they will probably be significant things like learning to read, dress themselves, make breakfast, take the bus to school, or look after a pet. Once they decide on what's significant for them, encourage them to choose a symbol representing this to place on the altar; for example, a book, a breakfast bowl, or a bus pass, along with more decorative items.

You will need:

- The altar itself; this can be simply a piece of floor (or ground, if you are outside) or an arrangement using boxes or tables. If you are short on space, a bookcase or coffee table can be converted, if only temporarily. Outside, you may choose a friendly rock, tree stump, or plank of wood for your altar

- A cloth or covering for the altar. Consider old sarongs, worn-out dresses, pieces of fabric, or colored wrapping paper; if you are outside, a layer of sand or leaves will work

- A back-panel or wall-decoration for the altar (not needed for altars you can approach from all sides). You may wish to create a painting or other decoration for the back of your altar

- Items to represent the harvest. This usually includes in-season vegetables, seedpods, autumn leaves, or more personal items

- Extra items for the altar such as statuettes of Gods or Goddesses, candles, and whatever else you like. Off-cut branches, fern fronds, or other foliage may be available from your garden

- A camera to photograph your finished altar (optional)

Time:

• 30 minutes

Intention

It's lovely before you begin creating the altar to spend a moment or two reflecting on your intention. Are you building it as a thanksgiving? As a reminder of the richness of your life? Perhaps you are creating this altar purely to celebrate autumn.

Method

Every altar is different. Allow creativity to guide it. Someone might begin creating it in the middle of the floor when you had planned for it elsewhere; or they might build a towering structure when you had imagined it neat and contained. If you are outside, you can build an altar in the sheltering crevices of a rock, around the base of a tree, or in a flower bed.

• Think about how to represent your intention as you create your altar. If your intention is to celebrate a time of plenty, you might want to include four or five pumpkins from your veggie patch instead of just one. If your intention is to honor your family, make sure representations of all the family members are on the altar.

• Making things for the altar can also be part of this process; in which case, allow longer than half an hour. You can add autumn collages of leaves, vegetables, or food you've cooked or preserved such as jars of chutney, biscuits, strings of chilies or garlic, or bunches of dried herbs. If your altar is outside, you may wish to leave gifts for those who come after you've left—offerings for the fairies or seed for birds.

• If you are dedicated to a particular God or Goddess, if there is one you would like to thank for their role in your life during the past year, or if you would like to invoke a particular God or

Goddess for the coming months, you can place an image
of them on the altar or a symbol representing them, or leave
a specially tailored offering. I might leave a shell for Aphrodite,
a handful of nuts for the Green Man, and a necklace for Freya.

- It's lovely to take photos of your altar when it's finished. You can
  share them with friends, possibly inspiring more Autumn Altars,
  or collect them over the years to show off all the different altars.
  You can also put it on your everyday altar or paste it into your
  journal or Book of Shadows.

Samhain

Samhain is celebrated on October 31 in the Northern Hemisphere and April 30 in the Southern Hemisphere.

Samhain

At the first Samhain (most commonly pronounced *Sow-en* or *Sow-ain*) we had in our new, unfinished house, it rained. Nine-year-old Damon devised a twisting journey through the house all by candlelight which involved climbing over rocks, through gaps in the walls between rooms, along pieces of veranda, and in and out of various doorways. It was the year we made shadow masks, displaying one of our shadow characteristics; mine was *Liar*. To begin, at the foot of the stairs we had to reveal our shadow name, put on the mask, and then slither up the staircase, under a low bar. We visited different realms, passed tests, and momentously entered into a room lit by a single candle that contained only a four-poster bed. A particularly tall man who had lived most of his sixty years outside and looked weather-beaten, angular, and ancient was lying in the bed, and Damon opened the door for us one by one, inviting us to visit with Death.

When I came in, Death was lying on his back on one side of the bed. I lay on the other side, also on my back. Neither of us spoke. It was peaceful and unnerving at the same time, this awareness of death—and even my own death—simply being present with it. Other people talked with Death, held hands with Death, and one man told us he had embraced Death. It was my bed, a new bed I had never slept in, and afterward I didn't sleep in it or in that room for many months. We had used a red sheet for him to lie on. It wasn't my sheet, but it was left at my house, and I could never bring myself to use it. Eventually it got ripped up and used for something else.

This experience of entering the realms of death is one we've courted at Samhain. We don't discourage children from attending; children usually love Samhain, dressing up and playing wild nighttime games, but we do ask parents to consider the themes of the ritual and discuss them with their children both before and after the ritual.

Often we've worked with a myth. On this night more than others there's a sense of abandon that creeps in, twisting the reenactment that extra step further than we planned. I vividly remember a Samhain where we were divided into attendants of Hades and attendants of Persephone. I happened to be outside with Persephone; when we came to enter the Underworld, courteously accompanied by Hades who was promising a cornucopia of riches if we undertook the journey, it was to discover they had created a three-dimensional obstacle course using all the furniture, built in huge tumbled shapes throughout the center of the darkened house. It was chaotic, with chairs balanced on top of everything, labyrinthine (involving crawling under some sections and climbing over others) and probably dangerous. But definitely mythic.

Every year we acknowledge and honor those who've died during the previous twelve months and create an altar for their photographs and mementos as well as lighting a candle for each one. One year we had half a dozen teenagers present and we happened to be outside. One of them named a friend who'd died in one of the several yearly tragic car accidents involving young men our rural area. He began weeping as he spoke of it, and then most of the others did as well. The sense of darkness and enormity grew. In that context, they allowed the adults to witness and comfort their grief. Once during the US war with Iraq, we laid out several hundred extra tea lights in triangular rays spreading out from the altar and while we read out civilian and military casualty statistics and snippets of reporting from that war, Damon knelt on the ground and lit each candle, one by one.

This yearly ceremony has been deeply moving for me, especially to acknowledge those I didn't know well or who were far away when they died— uncles or second cousins I have memories of from twenty years ago, someone whose face and presence I knew but not enough to call them a friend. And there have been people I knew well, and somehow it's reassuring to hear them named in that company of the barely known and unknown, to see each one assigned a candle, all alike at this stage. It brings the presence of death very clearly among the living as each year we gather up these names and bring them together. One year Trinda looked around at the children and said firmly, *We expect you to do this for us.*

Samhain Memoir

I have stepped off the stage of my old life and I am somewhere else, where everything will change. I am stepping between the worlds and things are translucent, shifting in veils and layers of meaning. It's Samhain, the Festival my birthday is closest to and the one I've always felt owned me whether I was in denial, resistance, or welcoming. Samhain always had its coils around me because I love traversing over the boundaries into the myth and magic this season is dedicated to. And even though it's death and closure, every ending meets a beginning. This time I can see the beginning. I am magical but becoming solid; walking the future path, taking up the turning of the Wheel, and traveling through it. I think my life is changing.

The weather has turned; it's colder and darker in the mornings. The year is closing in around us. At the same time, something is opening, expanding, creating itself, and this part of me that's been unmet for so long is reaching out. There's a man I always cared for and admired. He was different from the partners I'd had; solid, cheerful, and engaged with the world in a pragmatic and optimistic way but still with room for the personal realm. For a long time when I looked at men, I wondered if he would approve of them, like them. I wondered if they were a bit like him.

The last time I was overseas I dreamed of his death. I'd gone home, in the dream, and was walking down the street of our small town when I met someone I knew. We stopped to chat; she was keen to catch me up on all that had happened while I'd been away. She said his name and that he had died. I was horrified. *Yes*, she said, *everyone was shocked. It was completely unexpected*, and she kept talking while I was facing this great tearing emptiness. Still in the dream, I went home, unable to grapple properly with the news. Every moment I remembered it there was a huge screaming inside me, absolute denial and distress and loss. Far more loss than I could account for, really. When I woke up, it was still more than I could account for, but it was also seared into my memory. I resolved to tell him of the dream when I returned.

When I did return, I discovered his long-term relationship had ended. He was not dead, though he had been through a death. He was awkward when we met and said something abruptly, which I took to mean that even if I was the last woman on earth he would never be interested in me. We resumed a tentative friendship. Since I mentioned I was thinking of moving to the city, he emerged out of nowhere it seemed and began courting me. I am disbelieving, but watch the patterns swirl tight about us. I wanted someone like him—how much more like him could anyone get?

Now, at the very beginning of our relationship, it is Samhain. *Bring a piece of your heart as an entry price to the Underworld*, I wrote on the invitations. I've gone out and bought a beautiful soft, white, embroidered baby's smock. I have no baby to give it to; though I've struggled to give up the yearning to have another baby, I still hold some threads of it. If I choose this man, I will have to close that door; he will be the complete end to my baby possibilities. He's sixteen years older than I and his children are adults. I've carried it everywhere for days, this little smock, like parents carry their baby everywhere. It's too beautiful to give away; I can't imagine parting with it. Beginnings and endings, both at the same time.

In the ritual we cast the circle and call to the ancestors. Early on we name those who've died in the past twelve months—relatives, friends, and people from our community. For each one, we light a tea light and the number of flames grows; it seems each one of us knows two or three people who have died. Looking at the altar, the dead outnumber the living. This is the setting in which we prepare to head into the vortex of the Wheel, the place where everything vanishes, the living walk among the dead, and we can step into the spirit realms prior to the year being reborn a long eight weeks later at the Winter Solstice.

Trinda's made beautiful blank Fortune Cards, black with a stamped silver spiral on one side, white on the other. In colored pastels, we each draw our past year onto one of these cards. There are gardens, hearts, planes, sunrises, tears, and magic circles. Mine has a crescent moon on it, the red gate of a Japanese temple, one of my garden's endless lomandra, and some Beltaine ribbons down the side; my travel, my magic, my labor. We drop them all into the cauldron, leaving that year behind and offering ourselves to this night of spirits. We put our masks on and I lead everyone out the western doors into the night. Behind me I know the house is frantic with hidden, silent activity as Damon rolls up the heavy rugs and moves them out of the way while Trinda draws a chalk labyrinth on the concrete floor.

Outside it is a calm night; we are in silence now. We merge with the darkness of the garden, our masks meaning we are at least partly disguised from each other. It's hard to keep track of who's here and who's not, or if someone disappears or appears from our number. I lead the group around to the apex of the house, staring out into the darkest part of the night, and we begin our journeys inward to the realms of the dead. Those who prefer can meditate or gaze at the night sky. We have ten minutes to silently travel within and through the veils, seeking out those we love or those who come to us.

I am holding space for these journeys, so I don't travel myself but stare at the dark sky with its stars. The night sky is so powerful for me I am almost afraid of it; as a child, I wanted to learn more and more about those stars, more than any book would tell me. I am still fascinated by them as an adult; comets, stardust, cosmic beginnings, and dark matter, they glitter so brightly, pull so fiercely out into the unknown; it's that sky that tempts me to forget human, earthly life rather than any faery realm. I can imagine being lost there, in the universe and not knowing I was lost. I always loved those myths where people turn into stars, or traveled among the stars. I could probably stay out here forever.

As for the dead I've cared for, I remember to acknowledge them. My grandmother, who doesn't really seem dead to me but just a little further away; a distant great-aunt I was closer to than most people I've known; my best friend who was run over by a car when we were children; a friend who died from AIDS; a lovely local singer I heard many times; and a writer whose work I love. I breathe in the night and think gently of each one of them, holding them for a moment in my attention, my care. It seems enough to remember them in the garden, in the quiet spaces in between one part of the ritual and the next. Ten minutes standing like this is quite a long time, even with the backdrop of stars, which measure ages rather than minutes. Afterward, many people say it was their favorite part of the ritual.

Damon walks quietly up to me from the west so I know the house is ready. I begin the drum beat to call people back; back through the veils and also back from where they have spread out across the lawn or into the trees. No one notices Damon is added to our number, or that he wasn't there before; it's a night of shadows and anonymity. Gathered together we slowly progress around the front of the house toward the eastern doors and tromp noisily onto the wooden veranda. Trinda is there, standing at the entrance to the labyrinth as we flood inside and she croaks out that we may walk the labyrinth, one by one, and pay with a piece of our hearts when we reach the center. She tells us on the way out we are each to collect a card from the cauldron, for tonight is also a night of fortune telling and future-seeing.

I watch Damon lead the way first into the labyrinth and I see what his offering is—the piece of his heart; it's a small toy, surely representing his

childhood. How amazing, to watch my child deliberately leave his childhood behind in ritual, to see him acknowledging this. He used to say he
wanted to stay a child forever. But of course the Wheel turns, always and
endlessly, carrying him with it and at fifteen here he is, leaving one of his
toys in the center of the labyrinth, a piece of his heart.

Later I watch my beloved walk the labyrinth; the piece of his heart is
a last piece of his previous relationship. He said to me earlier, *What if I
just love you too much?* and of course I can't imagine such a thing, but some
of my fear has begun to lift; fear of being hurt, fear of risking everything
again. He walks steadily and I can't see in the dim light what it's like for
him in the center, if it costs him something to leave his past behind.

When it's my turn, I walk quickly and lightly through the labyrinth. I
am holding the little smock close, I don't want to give it up. I know I can't
have another baby—age, circumstance, choice—it hasn't happened and won't
happen now, but I don't want to give up this piece of fabric. I think of all the
things I've left behind in the labyrinth all those other years and none of them
seem as difficult as this; none to move me so surely further around the Wheel
into aging and beyond my current life. And of course each of us is doing that,
every time, it's just some times I count as more vivid than others.

Around and around I walk; the house is only lit by candles and I am
wearing a mask so no one can probably see the tears pouring down my face.
All these steps go only in one direction, and whichever way I am facing the
path still leads me to the center. Seemingly surrounded by all these different
paths, they are actually all one path; there's no choice. That is, infinite choice
remains, but only the path under my feet makes any sense. I had other possibilities—to move to the city, to pursue other romances—but once this
relationship was offered to me, all the paths realigned and this was the one I
was already on. I don't let my feet hesitate, but it seems a long journey and
I wouldn't mind if it kept going, if it means I don't have to reach the end.
It feels as if I am going to lay down the baby itself in the Underworld, not

just a smock. It feels like I will have to wrench it out of my body, force my hands to stop clutching it.

A turn, another turn, and another and now I am facing the low, small altar in the center; pieces of other peoples' hearts laid on it. I bend down, I squat beside it. I try to concentrate on what I am doing. I am folding up this piece of baby's clothing—unworn, never worn, not to be worn by any child of mine—folding it carefully and gently but loud in my head is a voice, a different voice from the one I was expecting. It says, *You have a beautiful child.*

Indeed, I know it absolutely. But this offering was not about him, but another little one I will never have, never hold in my arms or make up songs for. *You have a beautiful child,* I hear again and perhaps it is my own voice, dragging me past this moment; I stand up, facing the ring of masked others, and I've left behind my offering already, the piece of my heart. It's on the altar now and I can't have it back, ever. I take some steps out of the center. We're not winding back along the length of the labyrinth but stepping out of it to symbolize that we're still there, really, in the Underworld for a month or two while the Wheel turns from Samhain through to winter. We're deeply in and for a while before emerging.

After a few steps, I'm beside the cauldron and I reach in carelessly, not looking and not really thinking while I pull out a card. As soon as I look I know it's Damon's. I saw him drawing it. It's got pictures of the trip we went on—Ireland, Scotland, England, and Japan—all those special places and the companionship we shared. Our house is there, or I think that shape is meant to be our house, this austere, ambitious idea of a castle that we live in. He's got excitement of new beginnings flaring in the corners. He started mainstream school this year for the first time. *You have a beautiful child*—he is given to me and given to me again, in birth and life and now in this ritual.

I look up, but it's not his eyes I meet, though I'm clutching his card almost as closely as I held the white smock. This man who's come forward into my life is gazing at me, smiling at me, holding his hand out and waiting for me to come out of the labyrinth and go forward with him, into the rest of the ritual, the rest of the year, the rest of whatever is next. I gave up a baby—even an imaginary baby—and I am given back my son, and also a lover, partner, my beloved. Both of them living, and me living also. It's the night of mysteries and really I have no idea what will happen, but I'm able to walk forward.

Restoration of the Mysteries

Samhain is better known and still popularly celebrated as Halloween; it's the night of trick-or-treat, of masks and costumes, witches and ghosts. All Saints Day is the day after Samhain or Halloween, and All Souls Day the day after that. The Day of the Dead, the three-day Mexican festival, is also celebrated at this time. All commemorate the dead. They also share varying degrees of the idea that on this evening, these few days, or during this time of year, the veil between the worlds is thin and the realms of spirit and the ordinary world we live in overlap. Spirits can cross through in either direction; dead souls to move on, or return with a message for loved ones; or perhaps with more sinister purposes, as represented by the ghouls, ghosts, and demons of Halloween. One of the rituals of Samhain is that the living can also cross over into the realm of spirit. We wear disguises, or at least a mask, so our human form remains invisible to those we encounter.

It is the dying of the year and the leeching into winter. Autumn leaves have fallen, the last of the harvest has been gathered, and preparation for winter is under way. Seeing nature die back we are reminded of human death, especially recent deaths. The coming of winter also prompts an inward turn; it's more tempting to hurry home from work and pursue hobbies and activities that can be done inside. In contrast to the sociability of summer, many choose to spend winter quietly, dedicated to inward and family pursuits.

The Celts began their days at sunset, so their Festivals were celebrated on what we think of as the night before the event. Similarly, their year begins with the sunset of the year, what we might think of as its end point, Samhain. Between these two concepts—Samhain as the beginning of the year and Samhain as the end of the year—is the mystery of death and rebirth. It's about transformation; the time when the mysteries are at their deepest, yet paradoxically the moment we can access them. At this point the Wheel enters into death to emerge later into life again. In our world this symbolizes all we are starved of: deep spiritual questioning and journeying, communion with the mysteries, and initiation.

My strongest affiliation has been with the Dark Goddess, and my journeying into and out of her realms has emphasized for me what the basic structure of the Wheel shows: that descent into the dark is an inevitable and necessary part of the cycle. To resist the times and lessons of darkness is to be in resistance to the whole cycle, because the whole cannot function without this part. Our world has night as well as day, winter as well as summer, and death as well as birth. Relationships end exactly as often as they start, as many projects are completed or abandoned as are begun, and each life comes to a close. This is part of the cycle, just as night and sleep are part of our daily cycle.

And within night and sleep are many things we need. Whatever dreams may be—the brain sorting through the day's input, another life we live in reference to our innermost self, a communication between the conscious mind and unconscious—they are an intrinsic part of human life. Sleep is also a time for resting, healing, and growth. For most people, night is a time of relative freedom from the constrictions of the day; freedom for intimacy with a partner, with friends, with family. Social activities, lovemaking, and bonding with our children often occur in the evening hours. It's when we slip into our more private selves.

In spite of our dependence on dreams, night, and sleep, our society and culture do not make much space for intimacy or inwardness, and routinely avoid interacting with death and dying or any contemplation of these. We view them as finalities, end points. Following the Wheel of the Year we can see immediately this isn't so, that death and letting go are just one of eight segments and because the whole process is a circle, it is neither an end point nor a climax. Everything does die, and Samhain prompts a deeper understanding of this in offering it both as a transition stage, realizing we undergo regular periods of dying, as well as a larger picture, that while one or some lives end, others are born. So although dying is an end of *something*, it is never an *end*.

To recognize and honor this can bring deep healing to the fear and denial many of us experience around death. To step into a place where it is understood as part of the natural order—not just academically understood, but where it becomes a lived participation in the cycle—is to begin to shift deeply held prejudices and fears that cause us much extra pain when someone we love dies or we contemplate our own death. And this will radically alter our experience of those countless fallings-away we all experience through life, when we lose a job or opportunity we were attached to, a friendship or relationship comes to an end, or we face a health issue or other crisis.

Samhain is the ideal time for initiations, for finding one's place in the spirit realms, and for walking paths that are not of the everyday world. Initiation is like death, is modeled on death, where there's a stripping away of whatever has been (status, knowledge, or certainty) and entry into the unknown. But it is done with purpose, with intent. It's a liminal time, when things can permanently change. Even though it occurs at the very edges of ordinary experience, it catapults us into our own center, the core of who we are or who we are becoming. Initiations can mark life stages such as adulthood, marriage, and eldership, or they can mark levels of esoteric understanding, experience, or responsibility. Initiations work in both the inner and outer realms; they change one's understanding of oneself as well as one's relationship to the world. Along with death and dying, initiatory transitions are given short shrift in our world.

Initiations don't always look like much, on the outside. Anyone can be left alone in a cave for a night, be washed in the sea, or undergo a few days of fasting in the wilderness; an initiation is what's happening on the inside. During initiation, all our usual props are taken from us, often including our personal belongings, clothing, the name we are known by, familiarity with the surroundings, or knowledge of what is going to occur. Then we are tipped into the mythos, whether that be the mythos of a particular tribe, religion, or tradition, or our own personal mythos, that deep dwelling place of half-glimpsed understandings and divine presence where our true self, our soul, dwells. Within this mythos the cave becomes the womb of the earth mother, being washed in the sea is a rebirth, and fasting in the wilderness is an ecstatic return to nature. Symbols, words, and actions acquire enormous resonance, exactly as they would in a myth; we move through the landscape of initiation writing and rewriting the myth of ourselves.

Samhain is a time of layering—we've layered in the dying of the year with human deaths, both our own death, moving inevitably closer to us, and deaths of others we've known and loved. Adding a third layer by deliberately journeying into mythic or spirit realms within ritual deepens our connection to this season. There are many myths ideal for this journeying; Greek myths of Persephone descending into the Underworld, the minotaur in his labyrinth, and the Sumerian myth of Gilgamesh are three we've dedicated our Samhain rituals to. There are countless others that explore the themes and territory of the Underworld, initiation, and rebirth from every religion and culture I can think of.

When the doorway is opened to the other world—whether it be into Narnia, a land at the top of the Magic Faraway Tree, a portal into Fionavar, the opening pages of *The Lord of the Rings*, an invitation arriving by owl to attend Hogwarts, or any of hundreds of others—who can resist? When we read of Persephone, Orpheus, Inanna, or Theseus taking those first steps into the

Underworld, a part of us might hang back quivering and doubting, but the major part of us leaps forward into the unknown, the realms of mystery. When we are offered a few pomegranate seeds in ritual, which of us doesn't eat? When we are invited to step forward into the magic circle or over the threshold, who declines? Given the chance to dress as a monster, witch, or hobgoblin and rampage through the streets, what child turns it down?

We are filled with hunger for the mythic and we dare ourselves and each other, stepping forward eagerly to visit the minotaur in his labyrinth or meet the Dark Goddess in her Underworld. We know the only rule is that we will return changed and that change will be unknowable before it occurs; yet there we are on the path and nothing could hold us back. Why is that? Could it be that, like the children ecstatic to play ghouls and hobgoblins for tricks and treats on Halloween, we also are starving for the half-glimpsed realms this night provokes? We also long to break out of our tight confines and say goodbye to the ordinary by welcoming a ruthless stripping away of the polite, mundane, and everyday world. Send us on a journey! The journey of Gilgamesh seeking immortality, the journey of Theseus into the labyrinth, the journey of Persephone. And maybe those journeys will teach us something; not just the wonders of the mythic realm but something we can take back with us, to the ordinary. We will win a prize to replace what we sacrificed to make this journey. Seeking magic, wonder, and the unknown is always a dare and always involves leaving behind everything you already know and have— in fact, it demands leaving behind who you have been. Without this risk, this price, this necessity, nothing truly new can be discovered. Every time we take these journeys, we make discoveries.

We discover the great sadness of the minotaur, hidden away in his labyrinth. We learn of our own fear or our courage. We discover within the victory of Gilgamesh felling the forests of Lebanon his tragedy as he crosses his greatest friend, Enkidu, whose essentially wild nature cannot condone this act of destruction. We learn of the destroyer in ourselves and the part of us damaged by this. We learn—not secondhand from a book or story, but firsthand in our own bodies—Persephone's impatience, desire, curiosity, and daring as she picks the flower that opens the door into the Underworld. As we enter the myth, we see freshly. This is possible because, like in initiation, we leave behind our ordinary selves in order to step into the story. This leaving behind, passing into another realm, is the essence of Samhain. But this most hidden section of the year, played out in darkness in the realms of spirits and myths with masks and cloaks, is not a static state; it is the most dynamic and fertile ground.

It's the restoration of order. There has been plenty, growth, fullness, and abundance, and now is the time of balance, of stripping away everything or nearly everything, returning to a state of grace where once again things can begin. In the real world, we experience this as harsh or even unjust every time someone we love dies unexpectedly, every gain that we later lose (a job, relationship, or other benefit), and at every point of our own aging. But it is essential, an essential part of the Wheel. In ritual, we can understand not just the allure of this realm of transition and mystery but its necessity. Our contract with life has always involved death. We know that during our lives we will face death and the deaths of those whom we love many times. Giving birth to our children we know we are sending them on a journey that includes death.

Samhain shows us the profound nature of exploring other realms, secret knowledge, and our hidden selves. It offers the space to reverently and ritually let go of those parts of our lives that prevent us from moving on around the natural cycle. To release those who have died. To step forward into the unknown. To practice leaving behind our worldly selves. Without this, we cannot get to the Winter Solstice, which is the turning point toward light; the following Festival, Imbolc, the emergence of new life; and the Spring Equinox, where light will once again balance darkness and the year will swing toward summer. Without passing through Samhain, we will be ever stuck on this side of it, facing what we most fear: death, letting go, and transition.

It is precisely in this nothingness—the time between letting go and understanding what comes next—that insights, revelations, and internal changes occur. It happens in initiation. It happens when we stand in a Samhain ritual and whisper the names of our dead and light candles for them. It happens when we place that which it is time to release on the altar. It is when we are most vulnerable, most revealed, and truest to ourselves that we can most clearly and simply see that the shedding and letting go are natural, necessary, and obvious. Then we are able to perform them simply and with far less fuss than when we resist. In that moment of grace—of going with the natural cycle—we understand what resistance can never teach us.

These moments of revelation are accepted as a common part of death-beds. The secret that has to be told, the forgiveness that needs to be asked and granted, the love that can now be spoken—why do we wait our whole lives for this? What if we were regularly to meet this moment? What if, every year, we were to step into a time made sacred and acknowledged by all present and recognize the limits of our lives, releasing our attachments, and allowing ourselves to speak and do and know what has to be spoken, done, and known?

What if we were to greet Samhain and all that goes with it as enthusi-astically as small children greet Halloween, knowing that treats come with traversing the ordinary boundaries? What if we were to teach our children that life is not just an onward-and-upward slog of increasing knowledge, power, wealth, and achievements but also a constant letting go, redefining, mourn-ing, and recognition of what's lost and left behind; in fact, that life is a more or less a constant transition between increase and decrease, between light and dark, between inward and outward? What if we were to live knowing and act-ing upon this? That transformation is not something to be shunned, denied, postponed, or avoided, but is the essential piece, the heart of the mystery?

Samhain Ritual

Notes: "Ritual Basics" on page 295 covers many aspects of ritual, including grounding, casting circles, invocations, and participation.

Instructions for making the Samhain Fortune Cards exist more fully on page 291.

People bringing children need to know that death and the Underworld are the themes of the ritual, and they should discuss these with the children before they attend. One parent or guardian per child is a good ratio.

Section 9, "Entering the Underworld" is the central part of this ritual.

Ask everyone to bring:

- Photos and/or mementos of those who have died in the last twelve months

- Treats for the hobgoblins (if you have children at the ritual)— nice things to eat, shiny things, small magical things

- A mask

- A piece of your heart, as a price to enter the Underworld. Make it clear this is an offering and will not be returned

- A flashlight–if sections or the whole of your ritual will be done outside at night, it's great for everyone to have their own flashlight

- Food for the Samhain Feast, if you are having one

Other things needed for this ritual:

- A basket or other container for the hobgoblins, to hold their treats

- Blank Fortune Cards (we use a thick card that is black on one side, white on the other, cut it into uniform, card-shaped sizes, about 3.5 inches x 6 inches or 9 centimeters x 15 centimeters)

- Colored pens/pastels and colored markers to create the Fortune Cards

- A container for the Fortune Cards—cauldron, bowl, or box

- Chimes, drum, or another instrument you can use to gather the group together in the dark or outside

- A very simple altar for your Underworld (a cloth or a piece of timber, easily moved into place)

- A more elaborate altar to hold the mementos of the dead

- Tea lights—at least as many as there will be dead commemorated–allow about three per person expected at the ritual

- Some spare masks (colored cardboard ones you can get in packs for children's parties are fine)

- An Underworld—usually in a different location from where the rest of the ritual occurs. This can be a maze, labyrinth, separate room, or grove… whatever you devise

- A box of tissues is a good idea

Clothing suggestion:
- Black, with masks

Roles in ritual:

These can all be done by different people, or one or two people can take all or most of the roles, depending on how confident and experienced the group is:

- Casting the circle and calling directions, which can be done by several different people, or all by one person

- Invocations (optional)

- Grounding

- Leading warm-ups

- Leading discussion and giving instructions

- A hobgoblin leader (this can be a teenager or an adult, depending on the ages and maturity of the children and where they are—if they are at the front door there will be different requirements than if they are far away from the house)

- A guide for the journey into the spirit realms

- Several people to physically arrange the Underworld section of the ritual. This may be done before the ritual, if your Underworld is in a separate location (for example outside, while the rest of the ritual is inside, or the other way round) or during the segment of the ritual when everyone else goes on the journey to the spirit realms

- Timekeeper (this may not be necessary, or can be combined with another role)

- Drummer/song leader

Length of Ritual: 2 hours

Ritual

Pre-ritual hobgoblins: If you have children attending and are planning to have a hobgoblin group (which can be called something else), let parents know this is planned, and either drop their children off a little early, or arrange some way for the hobgoblins to collect their treats. Our hobgoblins waited up beside the gate, and refused people entry until the treats had been handed over. Lead hobgoblins should be clear on what to do with people who've forgotten to bring treats (they might extract IOUs, or suggest searching in pockets or in the car) and the hobgoblins need to know this is a token price and accept whatever is offered. Hobgoblin treats are distributed after the ritual.

1. Gathering

Welcome the group to the ritual space and take care of any housekeeping. If some people are unfamiliar with ritual etiquette, briefly explain how you'd like the ritual to run.

Include some information about masks; explain that they will be used later in the ritual and they are a symbolic way of transiting safely through spirit realms, speaking with the dead and entering the Underworld. Suggest that for the introduction and early parts of the ritual, masks are optional, but they are put on for the journey into the spirit realms and remain on for the majority of the ritual (people may prefer to take them off when you are singing and dancing at the end). They can also be ritually put on for the casting and final release of the circle.

Announce the intention of the ritual. This could be, *Tonight we're celebrating Samhain, the night when the veils between the worlds are thinnest, On this day we acknowledge and honor our dead,* or *Tonight we enter into the darkest part of the year.*

Ask everyone to introduce themselves briefly. Start with yourself to give a demonstration of the type of introduction you want. If you have a large group (over twenty), you can ask people simply to introduce themselves to the person or people next to them.

2. Grounding and Warm-ups

Warm-ups are optional, but great in a group that doesn't know each other well or isn't practiced in ritual, and also in groups with children. If the children have just been hobgoblins, you may need the warm-ups to function as a cooling-down process.

GROUNDING:

- Briefly introduce the idea of grounding; that it is done to assist everyone to become more present, feel alive in their bodies, and release distractions.

- Offer a seasonal grounding, such as being a tree strongly rooted in the ground and preparing for the cold season. Depending where you live, you may let leaves fall to the ground, feel sap slowing down, or other seasonal variations.

- Speak slowly and clearly, adding intonation and variety to your voice to assist and inspire those listening.

- Finish with a clear instruction for everyone to open their eyes (if they were shut) and become fully present.

SUGGESTED WARM-UPS:

- **Physical:** Body of the Mask; ask people to step into the circle one by one and create a whole body position (not just a face) that reflects their mask. Then everyone copies them.

- **Vocal:** Group toning; do some introductory breath work and then begin toning. Ask everyone to feel into the season and allow their voices and sounds to reflect that. Let the toning run for a couple of minutes, long enough to create a group sound that may rise and drop and take on its own characteristics.

3. Creating a Sacred Space

- **Cast a circle:** Have someone walk around the perimeter of your circle using their hand or a magical tool to outline the circle. They may tone or sing as they do this.

- **Call to the directions: and elements:** Call to eight directions if you can. Make sure each calling is succinct and powerful; otherwise, it becomes the opposite of a tight, energetic container. If you don't have enough people for this, call into the Cross-Quarters, as Samhain is a Cross-Quarter Festival. All together call Above and Below.

Northern Hemisphere:

Northeast	Beginnings, the first breath
East	(Air) Thought, sound, and word
Southeast	Stirrings, passion
South	(Fire) Fullness, power, and brightness
Southwest	Sacrifice, offerings
West	(Water) Completion, harvest
Northwest	Samhain, night of the spirits, and the other realms
North	(Earth) Darkness, rest, and rebirth

Above and Below

Southern Hemisphere:

Southeast	Beginnings, the first breath
East	(Air) Thought, sound, and word
Northeast	Stirrings, passion
North	(Fire) Fullness, power, and brightness
Northwest	Sacrifice, offerings
West	(Water) Completion, harvest
Southwest	Samhain, night of the spirits, and the other realms
South	(Earth) Darkness, rest, and rebirth
Above and Below	

• **Invocations:** If you wish to invoke the ancestors, now is the time to do it. You can invoke personal ancestors, tribal ancestors and guardians of the land, or spiritual ancestors. If you invoke more than one type of ancestor, you can have different people speaking each invocation.

4. Introducing Samhain

Because of the emotionality of this ritual, speaking of those who've recently died, as well as the power and common fear of or unfamiliarity with transiting through other realms, this explanation is very important. Cover at least these basics:

• Samhain is one of eight segments on the Wheel of the Year and it is the time when we acknowledge and honor death, dying, and the other realms.

• Ask that anyone uncomfortable with a section of the ritual wait to one side while that section is happening; no one leaves the gathering until the whole ritual is completed.

- Explain the use of masks in the ritual—what they mean, why you are using them, and also when you will wear them.

- Ask parents/guardians to remain with their children throughout the ritual.

- Explain that at this time of the year we enter the Underworld, but we don't leave it yet. The ritual will conclude with everyone still symbolically in the Underworld.

- If there will be outside sections of the ritual (or movement from one place to another), provide an outline of the activity.

- Explain the piece of each person's heart is an offering, and so it will *not* be returned at the end of the ritual. Check everyone has an offering. If not, during the Fortune Card-making section of the ritual they can make or find something that symbolizes a piece of their heart.

- Emphasize that clear instructions will be given at every stage of the ritual.

- You may like to ask for any questions. Stay practical and clear in your answers.

Then talk a little about the Festival and ask each person to contribute their own ideas about the season and Samhain. For them it may mean a change in the weather, an awareness of the coming winter, or a time to retreat or withdraw in some way. If it is a large group (over twenty people), you can break into smaller groups for this section.

You might wish to include in the discussion the aspect of Samhain as the time of dying and stripping away, asking in what way this is relevant in people's lives.

5. Learning the Chants

Introduce the chants you will be using later in the ritual. It's best to have two chants—one to sing at the altar of the dead after the commemorations and a different one to sing at the end after everyone has entered into the Underworld.

There are many chants on CDs, online, and in songbooks. You may also have favorite chants that are known to your group or a songwriter among you. Choose simple songs or chants that are true to the themes of your ritual and teach them to the group by singing them a couple of times and then teaching them line by line. It's useful to sing them through together at least eight or ten times, so when you begin singing later in the ritual everyone can easily join in without having to be retaught the words or the tune.

6. Commemorating the Dead

Introduce this section of the ritual, explaining it is to commemorate those who have died in the previous twelve months. You cannot really control this, and people will often light candles for people who've died much longer ago. I allow this, while continuing to emphasize this ceremony is for people who've died in the last year.

For each person who has died, someone steps forward to speak about them, place their photo or other token on the altar, and light a tea light. It's good to go first yourself or have someone else who is familiar with this process go first, setting an example of how to do it. Sometimes others will also want to speak about that person, and sometimes they also light a candle. Allow people to do whatever they feel is right—speak about the person twice, light two tea lights, or have multiple people speak of someone at one time. Children will often speak of and light a candle for a pet who has died. Sometimes people light candles for someone well known who's died. Some people have four or five candles to light and may do them all at once; others take a break between sharing about one death and another. Sometimes parents stand forward with a child or children to speak of and light a candle for a grandparent or another relative or friend.

Keep this section of the ritual moving; it is very powerful but can also stretch out if there are long pauses between people naming their dead. When there is a longish pause, ask if there is anyone else to be honored.

When you are all finished, begin your first song very quietly, singing in honor of those who have died. Allow it to strengthen, but it does not matter if it never gets particularly loud; this song is not about raising energy but about sending good wishes to the dead, holding compassion for each other, and creating a sense of completion and release of those relationships.

7. Making Year Fortune Cards

This activity is described fully on page 291, immediately after the ritual.

Explain that just as you released those who died in the previous year, now you are going to release whatever's happened to us in the previous twelve months as part of the stripping away process to be able to move forward into the next year. This will be a symbolic release by making a card that will be left behind before the next part of the ritual.

Bring out the cards and coloring things. Ask that color, shape, and symbols be used to convey a sense of the year; don't use words. Give a definite time for this activity, and a reminder a few minutes before you want everyone to be finished.

Place your cauldron, box, or basket in the center of the circle and have each person drop the card into it. You may like to say a few words of cleansing or dissolution over the cards, or smudge them or sound a chime over them.

8. Journeying to the Spirit Realms

I always make this a physical journey (outside or through different sections of a house); if space is very limited, you may have to lead it as a guided visualization. If this is the case, encourage everyone to stand or sit rather than lie down and emphasize the benefits of alertness. Transiting into the spirit realms is not the ideal time to let your attention wander or fall asleep.

Make sure everyone is wearing their mask and has their flashlight with them if you are going outside or wandering through a dark house. They also need their offering for the Underworld (small children can share in their parents' or guardians' offerings). Mention that everyone has a choice whether to step through the veils and seek out the dead; other alternatives are simply enjoying the night or meditating quietly.

It's best if the person leading this journey has practiced a few times to get a feeling for the timing, effective phrases, and clear instructions. Following is my suggested outline for the journey, but alter it to fit individual circumstances.

• When the group is gathered together, ask them to wear their masks and keep them on for the entire journey. Count the group.

• Lead the way outside or to the beginning place of the journey and give all the practical instructions—the route you are taking, how long this part of the ritual will take (usually ten to fifteen minutes, though you can spend longer on it if your group is made up of experienced ritualists), and clearly outline again the different choices of what people can do during this time.

• Give a demonstration of the method you will use to call the group back together when this stage of the ritual is finished, such as chimes or a drum beat.

• Taking the group with you, step into the night and lead them to a quiet, dark place.

• Lead in with a very short relaxation, becoming present to the night; then begin your (brief) description of reaching or stepping through the veils into the other realms.

• Remind everyone they can return completely to their own bodies at any time they choose.

- Give a time for the journey (around ten minutes) and announce you will be silent now to allow them to undertake their journeys, speak to loved ones, meditate, or just enjoy the night. They may choose to move away, although remaining within hearing distance.

- When the time is up, make your signal and gather your group, ensuring that all are present.

- Lead a short grounding in a few sentences and announce now, in these physical bodies, you will enter the Underworld. Walk with the group to the entry place for the Underworld.

9. Entering the Underworld

This will vary from ritual to ritual, depending if your Underworld is a maze, labyrinth, or another area. You may like to collect the entry price from people as they enter, or have them place it in the center once they arrive.

Have a guardian or gatekeeper (usually someone who was involved in creating the Underworld) announce the entry and the price for each person who seeks to enter—a piece of their heart.

Have something to do in the Underworld, such as walking a maze or labyrinth, meditating, or even dancing if there is room. Other options include meeting the Dark Goddess, or the Dark Lord, or Death; have each person perform a symbolic action or set of actions such as answering challenges; climbing over, under, or through obstacles; or eating a mouthful of Underworld food, which could be pomegranate seeds, ritually baked bread, or dark chocolate.

When each person has completed what needs to be done in the Underworld, have them pick a Fortune Card out of the cauldron, box, or basket as a token for the following year.

10. Raising Energy

The drummer, percussionist, or song leader should begin the song as soon as each person has been through the Underworld. Use a different song than the one you sang for the dead.

You may choose to raise a cone of power, run the chant as a round, or blend the chant with your earlier Samhain toning and sounds. Continue until it is obvious the energy and sound have peaked, and then let the sounds die away. Stay in silence a little longer than usual.

11. Sharing

For this ritual, it's best to have a sharing circle. If there are a lot of people, you can break into smaller groups, but make sure a person who created and held the ritual is in every group so if anything unresolved comes up it can be dealt with.

You can begin by asking people to briefly say what they make of their Fortune Card (or their fortune) for the coming year. Then ask them to comment on one aspect of the ritual that they found strongest.

An alternative is to have them explain the Fortune Card to the person next to them or in groups of three, and then come back to the whole group for the final comments on the ritual.

12. Complete the Circle

Honor and thank all those invoked. Acknowledge the directions in the reverse order that they were called and dissolve the circle. Generally the same people who did the calling, invocations, and casting do this. At Samhain it is worth giving an extra-special thank you to the hobgoblins (if you had them) and asking their energy to depart.

- **Acknowledge:** If you invoked the ancestors, now is the time to thank and acknowledge them and ask them respectfully to return to their own places.

- **Acknowledge the directions and elements:**

  Northern Hemisphere:
  Above and Below

North	(Earth) Darkness, rest, and rebirth
Northwest	Samhain, night of the spirits, and the other realms
West	(Water) Completion, harvest
Southwest	Sacrifice, offerings
South	(Fire) Fullness, power, and brightness
Southeast	Stirrings, passion
East	(Air) Thought, sound, and word
Northeast	Beginnings, the first breath

  Southern Hemisphere:
  Above and Below

South	(Earth) Darkness, rest, and rebirth
Southwest	Samhain, night of the spirits, and the other realms
West	(Water) Completion, harvest
Northwest	Sacrifice, offerings
North	(Fire) Fullness, power, and brightness
Northeast	Stirrings, passion
East	(Air) Thought, sound, and word
Southeast	Beginnings, the first breath

- **Dissolve the circle:** If a circle was cast, the same person walks around it in the opposite direction, gathering up the energy or otherwise dispersing it.

Thank everyone for coming and for the energy they have contributed.

It's important to chat individually with each person who came about how they found the ritual in case anyone is distressed or uncertain.

Divide up the hobgoblin treats.

Leave the Altar of the Dead there for the duration of your time together, but make sure people take their photos and mementos with them. Preferably, allow the tea lights on this altar to burn until they are finished. The pieces of people's heart that were the entry price to the Underworld should be buried, burned, or otherwise disposed of as appropriate after the ritual.

If you are having a Samhain Feast, before you begin eating ask the youngest child (or youngest practicable) to put together a small plate with a sample of every food present and place it on the altar as an offering for the dead.

Samhain Activity: Fortune Cards

These Fortune Cards are a little like Tarot cards; they can be used to predict aspects of the coming year or to suggest forward paths. You can make them as a segment within a larger ritual, with friends and family, or by yourself.

If you are making cards with six or more people, you only need make one each. For a smaller group, you could make two or three cards each (they can be simpler cards). If you are making them on your own, you can make any number you choose. If you make them by yourself, you may choose to offer them as gifts or a lucky dip for anyone who visits your house in the next week or so after you have taken one or more for your own fortune telling for the coming year.

The cards have two functions: to release what has happened during the past year and to foretell or offer direction for the coming year. Because of the foretelling aspect, it's important that no card carries only severe or bleak-looking imagery; instead seek to balance such images with what emerges from loss or crisis, whether that is (as some Tarot cards show) a green shoot emerging from a blackened countryside, a serpent discarding an old skin, or a sunrise happening over a distant hill.

You will need:

- Blank Fortune Cards (we used a thick poster board that was black on one side, white on the other, and cut it into uniform, card-shaped sizes, about 3.5 inches x 6 inches or 9 centimeters x 15 centimeters)

- Colored pens, pastels, and colored markers

- A container for the Fortune Cards such as a cauldron, bowl, or box

- A small altar or lit candle (optional)

- Items for a cleansing of the cards such as a smudge stick, drum or chimes, or tokens of the four elements such as a feather, candle, chalice, and earth (optional)

Time:

- 30 minutes or longer if you are making more than one card per person

Intention

The intention of the Samhain Fortune Cards is to be freed from the energy and events of the previous year. You may also like to let people name what they are clearing away or some of the events (welcome and unwelcome) that occurred in the previous twelve months.

Method

If you are working with a group, explain this is to release whatever has happened in the previous twelve months as part of the stripping away process in moving forward to the next year. This will be a symbolic release by drawing using color, shape, and symbol on the card. Afterward, each person will receive one of these Fortune Cards to be read as an indicator of the year to come.

- Suggest everyone takes a few moments to consider the main themes, events, and understandings of the previous year, and then find a way to represent that on their cards. Ask that written words not be used, but instead color, shape, and symbols convey what they experienced during the year. Children might need help remembering, although sometimes they have a clear idea of what they want to express and how to do it.

- If you are working by yourself or with a small group and are consequently making more than one card each, split your year's happenings onto different cards. For example, you may have one card with a series of red hearts and a winding path, representing flirtations or love interests; another card with a tree which has fruit or flowers on one side, representing a career that has some promising aspects; and a third card filled with vibrant colors and different shapes, representing a rich creative life.

- When the cards are completed, gather them into your cauldron or other container, emphasizing as they are placed into this container that you are releasing the energy of the previous twelve months.

- If you like, and especially if this is not part of a larger ritual where the cards undergo a different transformation, now is the time to do a cleansing over them. It's great to have everyone contribute to this. You can offer some suggestions and then let everyone do what feels right, or you can lead a more formal cleansing and blessing ritual. The cards can be smudged and words of release spoken over them, each person could being smudged in turn; the cards can be blessed by the elements with a different person offering a blessing for each of the elements; or each person could speak a few words of release.

- In a large group, have each person pick out one card for a foretelling for the coming year. If you are in a small group or by yourself and have made more than one card per person, each person can pick several cards. You don't have to use up all the cards; for example, if you had a group of four people and each person made three cards, you might pick only two each, lending a more random element. In this case, not every card is recycled. If you are working by yourself and made seven cards, you might pick out three for your fortune reading. Even though you will be getting your own cards back (and this sometimes happens in groups as well) look at the card with fresh eyes and read the symbols as potential for your future rather than what they meant in the past.

- Ask each person to speak about the card or cards they picked; they can ask for help from others if they like. Emphasize the cards offer only possibilities, and free will and choice always exist. If you are working by yourself, record your thoughts in your journal or Book of Shadows; you can paste the cards in as well.

Ritual Basics

The following are guidelines only. If you already have a different way of running rituals and casting circles, include aspects of ritual that I don't mention, or don't do certain things that I list, please feel free to continue with what works for you, or to read this section purely as reference. If you want more in-depth information than is provided here, countless books and websites offer many variations on all of these topics.

Who's Coming to the Ritual?

If you have a dozen people who've never been to a ritual before, the ritual needs to be different than if you're catering to a group who has been meeting and celebrating Festivals together for years. If you have children coming to your ritual, you probably need some exciting warm-up games, one or two especially child-oriented parts of your ritual, and several other pieces they can happily participate in. If you have parents with babies coming, elderly, or unwell people, don't expect them to stand up for two hours. If you have clearly specified "no children" or "women only" and someone turns up who's not in your chosen category, be prepared to deal with this. The most graceful way is accepting them if they came in good faith and adapting your ritual where necessary. This may not always be appropriate.

Involve everyone in the ritual through activities, discussion, songs, and dancing. Split up leadership roles among as many people as practical to make your ritual more open, accessible, and owned by the participants. Making sure people are comfortable and that challenging or new experiences occur in a supportive environment is part of running the ritual.

Make your expectations clear from the outset to minimize misunderstandings and assist you in creating the type of ritual you want. Ask people to turn their phones off, tell them how long the ritual will take, explain the basic outline of the ritual, and give instructions clearly and simply as you come to each activity, repeating the main points. If you want certain things observed throughout the ritual—for example, no chatting between activities, or that people don't leave the circle—make that clear at the outset and then be prepared to follow up (sometimes people forget) and bend a little (when someone needs an unscheduled toilet break).

Asking People to Bring Things

I ask people to bring things for every ritual. I ask them to bring offerings for altars, food to share, a gift for another person, ribbons for the Maypole, and mementos of the dead on Samhain. Asking people to bring things requires some energy and thought to go into their participation. This lessens the divide between those organizing the ritual and those turning up, and starts people thinking about the themes of the ritual at least an hour or two before they arrive.

If and when people don't bring these things, sometimes they miss out; if they don't have a ribbon, they can't dance the Maypole, though they can drum, sing, and dance. Someone who turns up without an offering for an altar can go outside and find an offering. If you continually ask people to bring things it becomes an expected part of a ritual. It also means costs are spread out among those coming. For some things only I keep spares, mainly if I think it will ruin the ritual if everyone doesn't have a particular thing, such as masks at Samhain.

Dress/Clothes/Costumes

I love it when everyone turns up to a Beltaine ritual wearing red, or at least a red shirt. I love being at Samhain in black with a mask and realizing I hardly know who's there, since it's hard to tell one black masked shape from another. I love the feeling that we're all doing something together, deliberately and consciously. We started the celebration before we got to the ritual by dressing for it. We can't wear our best clothes every time; instead, we must scrounge around for green and white, or purple or blue; the solidarity of the group and the dictates of the Festival are more important than our individual likes (*How can I wear a red top with a red skirt?* or *Yellow's never suited me*). For a casual group—one that doesn't meet all the time—it's an immediate identifying and unifying feature, and visually it makes an impact.

Participation

Participation is what makes a ritual come alive. It can also make it unpredictable. Some people are just bursting to teach their own songs, be the leader of any group in which they find themselves, and get to know everyone there. Others are much shyer, preferring to stay on the edges of things and reluctant to give an opinion or join in the singing. A strongly structured ritual can cater to all of these people. Building in some level of required participation, giving opportunities to participate more fully, setting guidelines, providing clear examples of what you want, and creating many different ways of participating (song, dance, verbal sharing, different ritual roles, or creative tasks) will ensure that people fully participate in your ritual.

Intentions and Instructions

At the beginning of any ritual it is invaluable to state the intention. If things get difficult, slow, or waylaid, return to the intention. Give clear instructions for each activity, including how long it will take and what you expect from the participants. If you divide people into pairs for an activity and have allowed five minutes, tell them how much time they have and give them a signal at the halfway point. If they are in groups to devise an enactment, tell them the purpose of the enactment, what the steps are, and how long they have.

As soon as people begin to participate, you lose tight control of the ritual. Whatever you have said, some people will do something different because they were not listening, didn't understand the instructions, or just want to do it their own way. Most will do their absolute best to do what's been asked of them. Clear intentions and clear instructions guide the individual pieces as well as the whole ritual.

Timing

I prefer rituals that begin on time, have clear timelines set for different activities, and don't go past an hour and a half or two hours for a very complex, involving ritual. Most activities have a tendency to run for much longer than planned, so having a timekeeper adhering to the time will help the ritual to not drag out. It's easy to lead a brief grounding and discover it took fifteen minutes instead of three minutes unless you have practiced beforehand and know what you are doing. When people are in pairs or small groups, indicate when they are halfway through their time to assist them in completing their activity in the time allowed. Long, slow rituals may be appropriate for certain circumstances with practiced ritualists, but they usually don't hold focus or the attention of those who are there. Rituals that are shorter with pace and varied activities means people will want to come again.

Altars

Altars are beautiful and emblematic. An Imbolc altar may be simple and sparse with a candle, a single flower, and a symbol of the God or Goddess; while an Autumn Equinox altar can be lush and filled to overflowing with fruits, vegetables, colored candles, statuettes, paintings, and other offerings. Altars convey themes and act as a focus for attention, both visually and energetically. People working together to create an altar is a very undemanding type of participation that anyone can be part of; it helps instill a feeling of ownership and belonging to the ritual.

You can have your altar in the center of the circle or to one side. I often place an altar in its corresponding direction (for example, at the Spring Equinox I would place it in the east). Sometimes I have the altar on a large, round, metal tray so I can move it during the ritual. You can ask people ahead of time to bring something for the altar, making sure you specify what you want, such as flowers for the Summer Solstice, grain for Lammas, or you can provide a selection of materials to choose from.

An outside altar can be easily constructed. On the beach, make an area of flattened sand with some shells, a feather or two, and a spiral drawn in the center. In a park or garden, use fallen leaves, a few flowers or seedpods, and anything else that comes to hand. In the forest, an altar can be made at the base of a tree. You can clear away these altars when you've finished or leave them as a gift to the surroundings and spirits. People who are less vocally expressive may deeply appreciate the chance to create an altar (as well as other tangible forms of ritual). Children love both indoor and outdoor altars when they can choose what to put on them.

Grounding

Groundings are a powerful and beautiful part of ritual. They offer an immediate connection between the individual and the living earth. For someone who has just come through traffic, is nervous or uncertain about attending a ritual, or is preoccupied with a work or relationship issue, groundings offer a short, immediate path into clarity and presence. They are not trances, and teaching people to leave their eyes open during a grounding (the object, after all, is to become fully present) may assist each person to learn how to experience ritual states. Speaking in a solid, clear voice will support this, rather than a trance-like floating voice.

Rituals lead to ecstatic immanence; they open doorways to the divine and other ways of seeing and experiencing life. However, these experiences are infinitely more valuable to us when they are encased within solid reality. People who are fully present are far less liable to accidents, distractions, and zoning out. Groundings should take only five or fewer minutes with an experienced group or a less-experienced group.

Always explain what you are doing, its purpose, and what you'd like. For example, *I'm going to start with a brief grounding, which is to allow everyone to become fully present for the ritual. This is the time to release any thoughts not connected to being here, and take a moment to feel into your body. Please keep your eyes open, breathe as fully as you can, and let whatever images or feelings my words conjure up in you allow you to connect to yourself and to the earth.*

I like groundings to be relevant to the ritual they precede. Grounding for the Spring Equinox may focus on the image of a tree putting out new leaves or an egg cracking open; Samhain grounding might focus on the night sky and the immensity of the universe. Brief examples of different groundings are given in the ritual sections of this book. Other people like to run the same one each time, so grounding becomes a habit that is easily invoked. Using a clear, strong voice, keeping your own eyes open and your feet firmly on the ground, remaining aware of the time, and looking around are tools to ensure those listening have the best opportunity to ground themselves.

Some rituals offer the option to ground or release the energy at the end. I have heard it suggested that perhaps we should practice holding more energy instead of releasing it as soon as we've found or raised it. This is something to consider. Try a few different approaches; ask people what they like and why and find out what works best for you and your group. I do make sure my dissolving of the circle is very strong and complete, and I begin this with an acknowledgement and thanks to Below, which involves crouching down and touching the earth. When the ritual has been particularly powerful or otherworldly, I make sure to check in with each person after the finish. We also share a meal at the conclusion of a Festival; eating and talking are both great ways of grounding.

Sacred Ground

Paganism holds that all ground—any ground—is sacred ground. Thus whether we are conducting our ritual in a beautiful forest, on a beach, in a park, in our living room, or on a city street, this ground under our feet or under the building is a sacred part of the living earth. Many places where we perform rituals have been (or still are) sacred ground to another culture, and not always that long ago. In Australia it has become standard practice to acknowledge this at many different events and places, not just in ritual. Taronga Zoo in Sydney makes an announcement each morning at opening time, acknowledging the Aboriginal tribes who lived there. It is appropriate and respectful to genuinely honor the spirits of the land, the indigenous cultures, and guardians and elders, past and present.

Casting and Dissolving a Circle

Casting a circle is a formal way of beginning a ritual. It announces you are now stepping into sacred space and the actions and intentions that unfold during this time are consciously operating in the spiritual realms as well as in ordinary reality. It asks each person to be true to themselves, and acts as a focus for the ritual. If you cast a circle at the beginning of a ritual you need to dissolve it at the end. Sometimes this is called "opening" a circle.

Releasing, dissolving, or dispersing the circle are less-confusing terms, and I have used casting and dissolving throughout this book.

Casting a circle is done in physical space, though this is usually considered symbolic. Even though you've cast a circle just big enough for twelve people to stand in, at various parts of the ritual we might move outside this space into the rest of the room or farther away but still be considered to be within the energetic circle that was cast. You can make a reference to this when you are casting the circle, extending it as far as you will need.

Traditionally, someone walks around the circle drawing an energetic line either at waist height, shoulder height, or with a magic tool pointed at the ground. They use their hand or a magical tool such as a feather, wand, or staff. They walk in silence, or speak or sing as they go. They may ask everyone to help by humming, singing, or turning to follow their movement, casting with their hands. Other ways of casting a circle include scattering a circle of flower petals, sand, flour, or anything else; drawing a circle of chalk, a rope, or ribbon or having people take hands one by one around the circle. If you are walking round the circle to cast it, make sure you finish in the same place you started so the ends meet.

Dissolving the circle should be done in a way similar to the casting. Walk back around the circle dispersing your energetic space; gather up your flower petals, ribbon, or let go of each other's hands; make a conscious—and sometimes spoken—movement back into ordinary time and space.

You can make your circle a sphere by finishing with casting Above, followed by Below, after you've gone around the perimeter of the circle. Some people prefer to cast to the Center, and others use Above, Below, and Center. Some people prefer to do this as they do the directions, not in the casting, and others do it both in the casting and with the directions. Try a few different ways, and see what works for you.

Directions

There are four directions. Or five, including the center. Or eight if you count the Cross-Quarters, or nine if you count the Cross-Quarters and the center.

Really, there are infinite directions. Usually we choose to name some of them, creating a container for our ritual. If your intention is to celebrate every Festival, it is relevant to cast the circle into eight directions (with Center, Above, and Below as optional). Begin either in the east (with the rising sun) or at the anchor point for your hemisphere (south for the Northern Hemisphere and north for the Southern Hemisphere). Continue sunwise (clockwise for the Northern Hemisphere and counterclockwise for the Southern Hemisphere). If you are calling to Center, Above, and Below, these are usually called last. At the end of the ritual, when you are dissolving the circle, thank and acknowledge the directions in the reverse order that you called them. Using a rattle, drum, or other instrument to punctuate your calling can add strength to the calling.

- **These are the correspondences for both hemispheres:**

  Northern Hemisphere:

North	Winter Solstice
Northeast	Imbolc
East	Spring Equinox
Southeast	Beltaine
South	Summer Solstice
Southwest	Lammas
West	Autumn Equinox
Northwest	Samhain

  Southern Hemisphere:

South	Winter Solstice
Southeast	Imbolc

East	Spring Equinox
Northeast	Beltaine
North	Summer Solstice
Northwest	Lammas
West	Autumn Equinox
Southwest	Samhain

I like to have different people calling to the different directions. For example, at the Summer Solstice you can have pairs or couples calling to each direction. Sometimes I might have a child calling to the east and progress in age around the circle. When calling to the directions, it's nice to turn to that direction and call out to it. This does require a loud, carrying voice, so people behind you can hear what you are saying. You can practice first to make sure everyone can be heard. Lifting your head up and back will help carry your voice. When you are calling to the direction, mention two or three specific things about that direction. When dissolving the circle, a simple honoring and recognition is appropriate rather than elaborate descriptions. Dismissing or saying farewell to the direction makes no sense to me; the direction was there before you called to it and will go on being there. It is only us who are changing our consciousness of it.

Elements

You can call to the elements as well as or instead of the directions. I generally combine them into one calling, but you don't have to. Some rituals may seem strongly elemental to you, and you can emphasize or focus entirely on the elements, while other rituals may seem more referenced to the directions. Elements exist everywhere and all around us. Air, for example, is impossible to confine to one direction. Elements also exist both before we call to them and after we've finished the ritual, so I don't think it makes any sense to invoke or dismiss them.

Some people and groups feel very strongly about which elements belong in which direction, others are more experimental. Again, when the elements are being called, speak a few of their characteristics. You can speak either literal characteristics such as light and heat or metaphoric characteristics such as passion and creativity. When the circle is being dissolved, focus on briefly honoring and thanking the element rather than reiterating its qualities. An exception to this could be when one of the elements has been very strongly present in the ritual and you wish to acknowledge that, for example, *Water, we honor the depth of emotion you have brought today.*

Calling to the elements—whether as part of the direction calling or not—is a major opportunity to begin embodying magic of the elements themselves into your ritual. Calling to all the elements in the same voice and in the same manner is defeating the point. The calling for fire should explode and burn and flicker. Water can drip and trickle and cascade and glide and ebb and flow. Air can whisper and sing and rush and sigh, and earth can resound, deep and strong and staccato. Your whole body should resonate with the energy of the element you are calling.

Invocations

Invocations are used to call Gods, Goddesses, spirits, or particular energies to grace or inform your ritual. Like the elements, I prefer to think of them as immanent and always present. Dismissing them when a ritual is finished seems bad manners to me, perhaps a leftover from Western Occult magic where beings from other realms are customarily summoned and dismissed. Invocations request their attention, and ask us to become more deeply aware of their energies and stories.

Whether you are invoking a named deity, a broad category of spirit beings, or a presence particular to you, consider what role you are offering them in the ritual. Invoking ten Goddesses to a ritual focused on Persephone is probably disorienting, unfocused, and rude. Invoking Persephone is relevant. Many people like to be very specific, and rather than just naming a Goddess or God they specify the aspects of the deity they are invoking. Thanking those same presences at the conclusion of your ritual is basic ritual etiquette and another part of returning to normal, post-ritual space.

This goes for energies or more general categories of beings you invoke as well. If you are invoking the ancestors, know your intention for doing so. If you invoke the fae, do you just like to feel they're around? Or are you planning to work with them or offer them some role in the ritual? Even with elements, being aware of what you're asking is wise. I've been at a Summer Solstice ritual where *the full power of fire* was invoked. Later in the ritual, the burning wheel of bracken could not be extinguished, so there was a comic interval while three or four booted men stamped vigorously on our offering to the sun, trying to put the flames out.

An individual can make the invocation or the whole group can invoke together through song, sounding, dance, or other means. Like calling to the elements, an effective invocation requires the energy of whatever or whomever you're invoking being expressed through the voice and body of the person doing the invocation. If you are calling for the Horned Lord, conjure up a sense of him and let him move your feet and body as a stag might; raise your arms toward antlers and call out to him in his forests.

An example of an invocation is: *I call to Persephone! Goddess who travels between two worlds; Persephone, I call to you! We invite you to our ritual. Persephone, maiden of the fields! Persephone, daughter of Demeter! Persephone, adventurer and risk taker! Persephone, Queen of the Underworld! We ask you to bring your beauty, compassion, and daring to our ritual so that we, too, will be bold enough to taste of the pomegranate when it is offered to us. Welcome, Persephone!*

Chants/Songs

I teach the chant early in the ritual. If people are still feeling separate and uncertain, it can draw them in; later when you start singing, everyone will know the song. This is far better than getting to a pitched point in the ritual where you want to raise energy and then have to stop to teach the chant, or worse, beginning the chant without having taught it and hoping people will pick it up through some kind of osmosis.

I'm not a singer, and teaching and leading chants was for many years the most challenging part of running a ritual for me. I took singing lessons to remind me of basics, increase my confidence, and get used to singing in front of others. I've come to see the positive side of this; because I don't sing particularly well, it encourages others who are not comfortable with singing. I always make the point that we are not here to sound beautiful, but to combine our energy with the group and the ritual.

I usually have people stand to sing and remind them to relax, bend their knees, wriggle a little, and take some deep breaths. I ask people to open their mouths and look at someone across the circle from them or toward the center of the circle to project sound. Often I begin with toning before teaching the words of the chant to assist people to lose their nervousness about making any noise at all and be reassured by the group's ability to sound musical.

Some places to find appropriate chants are:

- CDs, including Reclaiming's *Chants: Ritual Music* (1987) and *Second Chants: More Ritual Music* (1994); Jana Runnalls's *I Sing Her Praises* (1999); and Sharon Knight and T. Thorn Coyle's *Songs for the Strengthening Sun* (2009) and *Songs for the Waning Year* (2009).

- The Internet. For example, type "Pagan chants" or "Winter Solstice chants" into a search engine and find dozens of websites devoted to chants with the words listed. Some will have links to videos or recordings, or may include written music; you can also improvise your own tune.

- Books. Many books on Paganism and Wheel of the Year rituals include the author's own chants, sometimes with written music.

- You may have singers, musicians, and songwriters in your group who are willing to experiment with creating chants especially for your rituals. Encourage them!

Music, Movement, Raising Energy

These are essential to a ritual that isn't to be dull, uninspiring, purely trance-based, or solely ceremonial. There are many different ways to include movement and dance in your ritual, from Dances of Peace to wild, free dance accompanied by drumming to walking meditations and anything else you can think of. Music can be made with drums and shakers or any other instruments you have. Sometimes prerecorded music can work in a ritual.

Raising energy may be done through song, drumming, dance, or all three. It is often done as the conclusion to a ritual, though it may happen at an earlier point. Raising energy is where you work to deliberately focus all your sound and attention on creating a pool, a peak, or a cone of energy that is then released, usually to send your wishes or intention out into the universe. If you're not familiar with raising energy, practice by yourself or with a small group before you teach it to a larger group. Usually, though not always, the sound and tempo increases as you progress, finishing in a sustained single tone.

Festival Feasts

It's traditional to share food together at times of celebration. Having a meal together after a ritual allows a social component as well as allowing space for people to reflect, share, and ask questions about the ritual. It's lovely to say a blessing over the food before you begin.

Asking everyone to bring a dish of food to share creates an instant feast, although if you have a small group you may chose to have one or two cooks or providers each time. You can ask that the food people bring be seasonal, or create a theme for each of your feasts. Thus your Spring Equinox feast may be a feast of salads, your Autumn Equinox feast may be the traditional Harvest Feast, and your Samhain feast can celebrate food from your family, heritage, or lineage. If the ritual is to take place outside, you can ask that finger food be brought, or that people bring their own plates and cutlery. If you don't want alcohol at your feasts, mention this on your invitation.

Create Your Own Seasonal Ritual

There are many ways to create a ritual. This is one way. You can do it by yourself or with a few other people for a large, small, public, or private ritual. I create a new ritual each time, though some people prefer to use the same rituals every year. Often one activity becomes a centerpiece of a yearly Festival (such as dancing a Maypole at Beltaine), even though the ritual around it may change substantially from year to year. Listed here are the steps I undertake to create a ritual.

Ritual

1. Themes

I begin by jotting notes under three headings:

- The Festival being celebrated and its themes

- The local environment: season, weather, and events; broader political and social environment: current issues and events

- A personal snapshot: issues or themes that are strong for me or for the people I'm creating the ritual with (and particularly those that are true for more than one person or overlap with the points above)

2. Intent

Look for commonalities. What is happening under at least two of those headings, or maybe all three? These themes usually become the focus of the ritual.

Rather than representing world issues as they currently are, I often seek to provide some redress, so in a time of increased international warring I would be more drawn to a peace ritual. If it was also the equinox—a time of balance—and I was also experiencing some disruption in my personal life, my ideas of a peace ritual would be confirmed. From this, I allow a definite intent to arise, and record it.

3. Activities

The next step is to come up with several activities to explore the intent and themes; for a ritual taking about an hour and a half, two or three activities is enough. These activities should flow into each other, though one may be more important to the theme and take more time than the others. This then becomes the central activity around which the ritual is based. For the peace ritual, I may decide on three activities. They will be working in small groups to allow each person to examine the role of peace in their own lives, leading into a peace collage to be collectively created, and later hanging the collage somewhere public, culminating in an energy raising to send peace out into the world.

When choosing these activities, check that they encompass different types of participation; in this case, spoken (in the small groups), creative (the collage), and energetic (raising energy, which will be accomplished through song, dance, and drumming). Then map out the body of the ritual, including how those activities will be run, the length of time they will take, and any special requirements. For example, if I'm expecting children at the ritual, will they be in small groups with their parents or in their own group? If I'm expecting children, do I need someone to lead that group? And do I have drummers for the energy raising? How will I get materials for the collage? Will I supply them, or ask everyone to bring a few things? What will be done with the collage after we've made it?

4. Consolidate

Check that the initial inspirations and intention are clearly and fully conveyed by the major parts of the ritual. If not, you may choose to replace or change an activity to convey your themes more clearly. For example, I may feel that the ritual pieces in my example above together combine to a ritual that's a bit soft and fluffy, when originally I was talking about war. I may choose to include some recent war statistics and quotes from newspapers throughout the ritual, read out at different times to create a jarring effect and show that greater things are at stake than our peace of minds. I will also adjust the energy raising at the end to be targeted toward places and people experiencing wars and the aftereffects of wars; I will offer for anyone to call out the names of these places as we send the energy off.

5. Complete

Then encase the ritual, deciding on the type of circle that will be cast, what or who will be invoked, the chant or chants you will use, introductions, and a grounding. For the peace ritual, to further my point about war, I may incorporate mention of these countries experiencing war in the calling to the directions. I will focus particularly on the grounding as it may be an emotional ritual, and I want each person to feel quite strong and responsible within themselves. I will choose an upbeat and action-oriented chant; this is the point where we are raising energy and I don't want anything slow or dirge-like.

I want the circle held strongly and clearly, so I will ask four people to call to the directions. For contrast, and because peace and war are issues that affect the future world, I will ask some children to cast the circle. I will ask everyone together to call Above (the divine) and Below (the sacred ground). I am largely relying on human agency to change this situation, and so I have decided not to invoke any Gods. Instead I will invoke some human qualities: courage, strength, clear vision, and empowerment. I will ask one person to stand in the center of the circle after the casting and directions and invoke these qualities into the ritual and invite each person to participate in them.

6. Extras

I decide what I will ask each person to bring with them to the ritual, what (if anything) I will ask them to wear, and what roles I'd like filled.

In this case, I will ask everyone to bring things to contribute to the collage: paints, ribbons, off-cuts of fabric, beads, and glitter glue. I will supply the backing piece of fabric.

For clothing, I feel that pure white—a standard, peaceful color—is too passive for the ritual, and instead ask people to wear mainly white, with a single bright color (to convey our life force, diversity, and vibrant power). These colors will also pick up on other themes of the Spring Equinox, new life bursting forth, and a reminder of the colored eggs we often paint or buy.

I'll ask whichever children are there to cast the circle, other people to call to the four quarters, invoke the qualities, run the warm-ups, grounding, and teach and lead the song. I'll ask one person to read out all the war statistics at the different stages throughout the ritual and another person to take responsibility for guiding the creation of the collage. I will do the welcome and intent, lead the discussion, and explain the different activities as we go through the ritual.

7. Check

Finally, I check through the written ritual, piece by piece, including the beginning and ending pieces, working out how long each piece will take and assigning times to different sections. If it is too long, I cut or reduce something; in this case, the small discussion groups will have to become pairs and take only about five minutes instead of twenty minutes. Having some idea of how many people will be there assists this, I have written out the timing as if I were expecting about fifteen people to attend.

The ritual now looks like this:

Spring Equinox Peace Ritual

Intention: *To realize our power to weight the balance toward peace in the world.*

- Welcome and ritual etiquette (2 minutes)

- Warm-ups (5 minutes)

- Grounding: strong, embodied (5 minutes)

- Cast circle: children (establish method), call to directions (two men, two women), referencing places of war and unrest; Above and Below (everyone) and calling qualities into center (one person) (total 10 minutes)

- Introduction to ritual: intention, names, discussion of Spring Equinox (15 minutes)

- Interrupter: someone reads out some statistics/news items (1 minute)

- Teach song and practice (5 minutes)

- Describe ritual and explain pair activity (3 minutes)

- Interrupter: someone reads out some statistics/news items (1 minute)

- Pairs, examining peace and war in our own lives (5 minutes)

- Collage set-up and intention (3 minutes)

- Creation of collage by whole group (20 minutes)

- Interrupter: someone reads out some statistics/news items (1 minute)

- Give instructions for energy raising (1 minute)

- Energy raising: song, leading to dance, culminating in sending off energy (10 minutes)

- Silence (1 minute)

- Below and Above thanked, four directions thanked, and circle dissolved (5 minutes)

- Total 92 minutes, or just over an hour and a half

Creating rituals is learned both in the planning stages and on the ground, as it's happening. Adaptability, creativity, and a sense of humor are all extremely helpful. For a group ritual, other people's input, support, and participation are essential. As you continue creating and holding rituals, you'll learn what works for you and the group as well as how and where your rituals can grow. One of the primary purposes of seasonal rituals is celebration, so if everyone's having a great time even though the ritual's diverged from the track you carefully devised, it may still be a very successful ritual.

Conclusion

The Wheel of the Year is also the Wheel of Life. As the Wheel turns through the year and through the years, we can watch the ever-unfolding cycles of nature in trees, birds, our vegetable gardens and the food on our tables, the weather, the place of the rising sun and its arc through the sky, the length of days, the lives of our children, our communities, and our own life. We can participate actively in these cycles by setting aside regular times to celebrate new beginnings, blossoming, maturation, completion, and resolution not just of each year and each life but also of our projects, careers, relationships, and spiritual practices. The Eight Festivals accord equal weight to each of these aspects.

The Wheel of Eight Festivals has been a great teacher for me. It has shown me how to create meaningful celebrations with my child and my community. It has inspired me to travel deeper and deeper into the cyclic journeys of nature, ritual, and myth. It has supported me in building understanding of the place that darkness has—that loss, difficulties, and crisis have within the patterns of our lives. It has taught me to trust, and to value equally each learning and each phase and part of life. There have been times when I despaired at having no teacher in my life, and at those times I have felt the Wheel beckon to me, whisper to me, and brush against the edges of my awareness. Into its great mysteries and great simplicity I have allowed myself to sink, experiencing the Wheel as vast, immanent, and embracing. It has taken me with it on its turnings, again and again into the mysteries of each Festival and it has provided a framework for many personal and spiritual understandings as well as my son's growing up.

This Wheel and these Eight Festivals exist everywhere all over the world, in cities and outside cities regardless of country, culture, or dominant religion and in spite of whatever may be happening in your own life. By teaching of the earth's relationship to the sun, they speak of our relationship to the earth, to her growings, her dyings and her turnings. The Festivals teach us to find hope in the darkest places, to explore our wildness, mourn our losses and honor our grieving, revel in the fullness of life, appreciate our harvests, and create balance where it is needed. They encourage us to pay more attention to the natural cycles in our location and to appreciate them not just in passing but as markers for understanding the depths of our lives.

The Wheel honors, guides, holds, and contains the great journey of life we are embarked on. Its great lesson is of balance—the practical understandings of night balancing day, winter balancing summer, rest and release, and death balancing growth and birth. That understanding may contain the seeds that could turn our world around from its ceaseless upward and outward path that threatens to destroy fragile ecosystems, the weather of our planet, species threatened with extinction, oceans threatened with pollution, global warming, and forests threatened with desertification. Our culture's great fear of the dark might begin to be questioned if in our own lives we honored that half of the wheel as deeply and deliberately as we honored the bright half. We might have a hope to turn around our current direction of relentless destruction toward endless gain to one of living in harmony with our own planet if we brought celebration to all seasons of our own, our children's, and our community's lives.

At the Winter Solstice, as the sun turns back toward the earth, the light is born again within each one of us. We see this light when we look at our children or the children of our community, when we emerge from a dark place in our lives into new understanding, and each time a new beginning seizes hold of us.

At Imbolc, we observe that the days have become longer. We choose to invest our hope and energy into projects, relationships, and work without knowing how successful they will be. We understand this hope embodies the life force, even in difficulty and uncertainty.

By the time of the Spring Equinox, day and night are of equal length. Life is burgeoning all around us and we wholeheartedly celebrate its wonders, as we tip over the balance toward summer.

At Beltaine, we feel the energy rising, called forth by the effects of the strengthening sun in the trees and plants. We dance and play with our sensuality, reveling in our fertility of mind, flesh, and spirit as we join in the celebration.

The Summer Solstice is welcomed, arriving amid fruit and flowers as nature and the length of day reach their peak. We acknowledge union in our lives; within community, family, relationship, and with the earth itself.

By Lammas, we sense the shift toward the downward tilt of the year. We prepare for our harvests, looking forward to success. We offer our energy whole-heartedly to the work that needs to be done.

At the Autumn Equinox, we recognize another day of balance and further shifting toward the darker part of the year. We have gathered our harvest and celebrate it in feasting and plenty with those we love.

Samhain arrives and we honor our dead. We prepare ourselves to journey within, sacrificing or laying aside anything that no longer serves us. We choose to walk into the darkness, knowing what awaits us is transformation and rebirth.

Recommended Reading

Bodsworth, Roxanne T. *Sunwyse: Celebrating the Sacred Wheel of the Year in Australia*. Burwood, Austalia: Hihorse Publishing, 2003.

Cole, Jennifer. *Ceremonies of the Seasons: Exploring and Celebrating Nature's Eternal Cycles*. London: Duncan Baird Publishers, 2007.

Eight Festivals. Tara Celebrations, http://www.taracelebrations.org.

Ferguson, Diana. *The Magickal Year: A Pagan Perspective on the Natural World*. York Beach, ME: Samuel Weiser, 1996.

Heath, Robin. *Sun, Moon & Earth*. Glastonbury, Wales: Wooden Books, 1999.

Jones, Evan John, and Chas S. Clifton. *Sacred Mask Sacred Dance*. St. Paul, MN: Llewellyn, 1997.

Matthews, John. *The Summer Solstice: Celebrating the Journey of the Sun from May Day to Harvest*. Wheaton, IL: Quest Books, 2002.

McCoy, Edain. *The Sabbats: A Witch's Approach to Living the Old Ways.* St. Paul, MN: Llewellyn, 2001.

Restall Orr, Emma. *Spirits of the Sacred Grove: The World of a Druid Priestess.* London: Thorsons, 1998.

Starhawk, Diane Baker, and Anne Hill. *Circle Round: Raising Children in Goddess Traditions.* New York: Bantam, 2000.

Starhawk. *The Earth Path: Grounding Your Spirit in the Rhythms of Nature.* New York: HarperCollins, 2005.

Szirom, Tricia. *Seasons of the Goddess: Perspectives from the Southern Hemisphere.* Melbourne, Australia: Gaia's Garden, 2011.